D0560268

AMERICAN MARKETING ASSOCIATION

The Co-Marketing Solution

STRATEGIC MARKETING THROUGH

- Better Branding
- Improved Trade Relationships
- Superior Promotions
- Effective Fact-Based Selling
- Accurate ROI Analyses of Trade Spending

Shawn Clark

NTC Business Books
NTC/Contemporary Publishing Group

Library of Congress Cataloging-in-Publication Data

Clark, Shawn.
The co-marketing solution: strategic marketing through better branding, improved trade relationships, superior promotions, effective fact-based selling, accurate ROI analyses of trade spending / Shawn Clark.
p. cm.
Includes bibliographical references and index.
ISBN 0-658-00006-3
1. Marketing—United States—Management. I. Title.
HF5415.13.C548 2000
658.8'02—dc21 99-38467
CIP

Interior design by Hespenheide Design

Published by NTC Business Books in conjunction with the American Marketing Association
A division of NTC/Contemporary Publishing Group, Inc.
4255 West Touhy Avenue, Lincolnwood (Chicago), Illinois 60712-1975 U.S.A.

Printed in the United States of America
International Standard Book Number: 0-658-00006-3
00 01 02 03 04 05 LB 19 18 17 16 15 14 13 12 11 10 9 8 7 6 5 4 3 2 1

To my loving wife, Susan, and my beautiful children, Cory, Chelsea, and Jodi, whose love and support made this book possible

Contents

Preface

I am a marketing man. As such, I have spent over a quarter century in the study, analysis, and on-the-job training in the use of the five Ps of marketing—price, perception, positioning, packaging, and promotion—to create a higher perceived value. A higher perceived value is what marketing is all about, because it leads to increased market share and profit. Also, much of my work has been in the areas of branding and brand management. Successful branding creates the most rewarding business results: a competitive barrier to entry and a higher return on assets.

I learned early in my career that fleeting business success can come from being in the right place at the right time with an emerging hot product or technology. Lasting success, however, requires learning how to leverage the hot product into a lasting business culture. Compare Osborne Computer, who introduced the first laptop computer, to Compaq Computer, who attained long-term success. Some companies, such as Procter & Gamble and Phillip Morris, institutionalized this type of success into a corporate culture. In attempting to understand how they did so, I was repeatedly led back to the basics of product branding along with fact-based, integrated market planning.

When the groundbreaking book *The Best and the Brightest* was the rage, I carefully studied the results of the different management styles presented. My research on the book's highlighted companies' returns on assets revealed that companies able to grow assets at a compound rate of 10 percent or more, such as Johnson & Johnson, were in the minority. In fact, some of those selected in the book had negative return-on-asset results! What was Johnson & Johnson doing differently from the other featured companies? The answer was brand management—and an almost fanatical emphasis on managing from a market-driven perspective.

Over the years I was able to piece together an unusual marketing career by jumping from one interesting situation to another. While most of my colleagues focused on advancing though the corporate ranks to the vice president level, I focused on job experiences that would increase my knowledge. My experience-hopping strategy led me to some world-class situations with leading consumer-marketing companies like Johnson & Johnson, H.J. Heinz, Hunt-Wesson Inc., and RJR Nabisco, where the execution of the brand-marketing model led to astonishing business results. Some of these—Heinz Ketchup, Johnson & Johnson Baby Shampoo, and Intel Inside—are recounted at length in the body of this book.

Of course, not every marketing adventure I followed ended in success. In fact, one particular failure proved especially instructive. Experiencing the unsuccessful $100 million launch of a natural cigarette, Real cigarette, may have taught me more than I learned from many of the successes I experienced. Living through a major marketing failure not only results in humility but also contributes more definitive knowledge about the proper use of marketing tools than is evident during the successes. Finding consensus about why a success occurred is often difficult. When all the marketing dynamics are properly in place, the result is often more than the sum of the component parts. Success seems to beget success, creating a momentum that extends beyond the isolated contribution of each component part. Analysis of a failure, on the other hand, can lead to the isolation of the marketing component that failed. This helps clarify the causal linkage between marketing action and result. In the case of Real cigarette, R.J. Reynolds was willing to spend the time and money necessary to conduct such a postmortem analysis, further adding to my growing store of marketing knowledge.

After serving about ten years in the marketing trenches, I graduated to the world of corporate strategy. My math training led me to become the marketing representative on a three-person team challenged to mathematically correlate the trends in the world economy with business strategies. We spent eighteen months and over $20 million on research to finally answer the posed questions and explain with mathematical confidence the underlying trends affecting our business environment. This opportunity to analyze and model the different marketing elements proved to be an invaluable way to separate the facts from all existing marketing lore. Armed with this information, I decided to witness firsthand how it could be applied in business situations other than packaged-goods marketing.

First, I worked in a retail environment, where we successfully adapted the brand-marketing principles to reposition a struggling auto parts chain. Next, I opened a consulting firm in which I worked with over 150 small, fast-growing entrepreneurial enterprises, many of which were in the technology field.

Operating as a vice president of marketing for hire, I devised branding and positioning strategies for numerous businesses in many nonrelated marketplaces. Eventually, this work led me to a $7 million claims-processing company that had helped develop and was then administering the most successful cooperative (co-op) advertising program of all time, Intel Inside. That program created for Intel in just 18 months the same level of consumer brand awareness that it took NutraSweet 18 years to develop, and Intel did so almost exclusively through the use of co-op advertising!

Of course, I already knew what co-op advertising was and something about the way it worked. But the term *co-op* was rarely mentioned during the ten years I spent working at director-level marketing positions with four Fortune 500 companies. In my retail work I had used co-op funds to offset part of the cost of my marketing campaign. But at that time I did not realize the enormous amount of money involved in co-op. My experience working with MediaNet that administered the payment of these funds for about 20 Fortune 500 companies was eye-opening, to say the least.

Billions and billions of manufacturers' dollars are spent by the trade, but very few actually promote any consumer demand or build store traffic. After spending over four years working exclusively with forward-looking companies to reengineer the use of these dollars to meet defined marketing objectives, I found that the dollars spent in this area are usually larger than the consumer-marketing budgets. And surprisingly, there are no marketing people involved in the planning or administration of these trade-marketing funds! This overlooked source of marketing funds represents a major opportunity for any company willing to invest in systems and management directives to manage trade-marketing funds properly.

In this book I recount what I have learned about applying brand-marketing principles to co-op and related spending areas. I do my utmost to show that a hidden opportunity exists for those marketers who take a proactive stance in using these funds to advance their marketing reach and develop co-marketing relationships with willing channel partners. This book identifies the scope of the co-op problem and describes in detail methods to take advantage of the opportunity co-marketing presents.

Finally, I would like to claim any errors or omissions in the final manuscript as my own. Some client information presented has been changed to avoid disclosing any confidential data.

Acknowledgments

Many people and organizations have contributed to the development of the Co-Marketing Solution. First, I want to thank ACS TradeOne Marketing and its many fine managers who helped me strap market planning on the front ends of their systems and market reporting and analysis on the back ends. I also wish to thank Affiliated Computer Services, the parent company of TradeOne Marketing, for their belief and investment in the Co-Marketing Solution. Without their willing assistance, it would not have been possible to develop and test the Co-Marketing Solution. Next, I would like to thank my good friends Bob Schwartz and David Stewart for their help in editing the original manuscript and Teri Driscoll for her skillful assistance with the final manuscript.

I am also indebted to the ACS TradeOne Marketing clients who were innovative enough to participate in a new approach to co-op advertising. Managers at companies like Intel, Sealy Mattress, Harley-Davidson, 3M, Motorola, and GTE Wireless provided invaluable opportunities to experiment with different aspects of the Co-Marketing Solution in the real world. Their belief in a higher vision for co-op made this book possible. And finally, I would like to thank Kent Stewart, Byron Marsales, and Victor Livingston, whose vigilant efforts made it possible to implement the Co-Marketing Solution on numerous occasions.

Introduction

You may have seen the TV spot in which a well-known style consultant trumpets the "great prices in quality clothes" at Target stores. With a winning smile, she assures the viewer that at Target, you can look great for less. Seconds later, the style consultant recommends using liquid Tide to clean those clothes. The spot implies that at Target, you'll find the right clothes *and* Tide, the right detergent to keep those clothes looking new.

Whose ad is this anyway? Is it a Tide commercial or a Target commercial? It is both. This TV spot illustrates the power and efficiency created when a manufacturer and a retailer partner in a message to the consumer. This type of strategically aligned brand promotion between retailer and manufacturer is a relatively new practice called co-marketing.

When executed properly, co-marketing promotions make it nearly impossible to tell whether the manufacturer or the retailer directed the effort. In fact, co-marketing programs are collaborative efforts. This way, the manufacturer and retailer ensure that the marketing message delivered to the end user is consistent with the branding goals of both parties.

In the TV spot, Target promotes its quality; Tide promotes its relationship with Target. The logical conclusion is that Tide is a quality product. Target and Tide are both linked to quality and to each other. If you need Tide, purchase it at Target. If you're at Target, remember to pick up the Tide. The retailer and manufacturer work hand in hand to boost sales. While co-marketing appears to be a logical way for manufacturers and retailers to spread brand messages and drive sales, this new form of partnership advertising stands in stark contrast to the age-old practice of cooperative advertising and trade marketing.

Cooperative advertising, often called co-op, has been around for over 50 years. The most common example of co-op is when a grocery store advertises a variety of different products and their prices in the newspaper. Typically, the manufacturer of each product pays for a portion of the advertising cost through a co-op advertising fund. The grocery store pays the remainder. In nearly every retail ad that promotes a product at a specific price, co-op is involved. But co-op dollars and trade marketing aren't just for advertising. Co-op advertising funds also are used to pay for those displays that you bump into on the supermarket aisle and the circular that's mailed or delivered to your house. Manufacturers also advance trade-marketing funds to pay for such things as permanent displays, stocking allowances, sales incentives, selling materials, store banners, even temporary price reductions. Anything that might help a retailer or distributor to sell, display, or advertise a product is probably paid for through the trade-marketing budget. Other expenses like trade shows or buyer trips and golf outings also are paid out of these funds. If you're getting the image of a poorly managed slush fund, you are not far off.

Trade marketing is a multibillion-dollar-a-year concern. For a number of reasons, the exact amount spent on co-op remains a matter of conjecture. Currently, it is estimated that U.S. companies spend from $40 to $55 billion a year on all trade-marketing efforts. Co-op advertising comprises about $15 billion of this total.

These figures illustrate two important points about co-op advertising. First, the great size of this advertising category indicates that nearly all manufacturers and service companies (or at least, all those who rely on someone else to sell their products) use co-op. Second, the inexact nature of the estimates suggests that these companies are not keeping track of their co-op advertising and overall trade-marketing expenditures the way one might expect. The second point is particularly difficult to understand and is, to a large degree, the reason this book needed to be written.

The divide between consumer and trade marketing might be likened to the difference between the executive's and janitor's washrooms. Executives at Fortune 1000 companies do not pinch pennies when it comes to honing the right message for their consumer-marketing campaigns. They invest millions on market research and testing before they approve advertising to be aired. At those same companies, the very same executives have little knowledge of the content, effectiveness, or efficiency of the product messages being delivered via co-op. These executives appear to be indifferent to the fate of co-op dollars, while elsewhere within the organization managers blindly authorize the expenditure of tens of millions of dollars on co-op advertising and trade promotions.

Ignorance appears to be bliss when it comes to trade marketing. But there is no bliss in the realization that American companies are losing track of an estimated $55 billion each year between their co-op advertising and trade-marketing expenditures. On the corporate level, most corporate finance executives would be surprised to find that between 3 and 5 percent of "top-line" sales is spent so carelessly. Some senior marketing types are recognizing that those spending dollars are often larger than their consumer budgets. More important, they are realizing these funds are spent without regard to the overall marketing goals and strategies of the organization. In fact, many times the trade-marketing messages contradict consumer-marketing messages. In a classic case of the tail wagging the dog, co-op programs are often driven by the desires of the retailer, and in some cases appear akin to knee-jerk reactions, occurring spontaneously without consciousness. The opportunity to introduce an integrated marketing approach to the situation cannot be overstated.

This book is written for all corporate executives, not just those directly involved in co-op and trade marketing. Although program administrators and salespeople man the front lines of trade marketing, they are not the only target readers of this book. This book is also for top-level executives—chief executives, financial officers, marketing people, and marketing strategists—who have the capabilities of changing the corporate culture and the responsibility of maximizing the bottom line.

Executives long seduced by the glamour of consumer marketing may learn that there is gold to be found in trade advertising. The old golf adage amended might read: "Consumer ads for show, trade ads for dough." By turning their attention to long-ignored co-op programs, those responsible for expenditures, profit, and shareholder value will be surprised by the major opportunity afforded by a co-marketing approach to trade spending.

Key executives will then begin to invest nearly as much time, money, and talent in the trade marketing arena as they do in consumer marketing. Executives may learn that the careful up-front planning and follow-up research attendant to any national television campaign would pay handsome dividends in trade advertising as well.

While there is no doubt that traditional co-op advertising can and does work (see my former colleague Bob Houk's book, *Co-op Advertising*, Lincolnwood, IL: NTC/Contemporary Publishing, 1995), here the question is: How can the effectiveness of trade-related advertising and promotional dollars be maximized? The answer lies in replacing the often times adversarial tactics of co-op advertising with the strategy of co-marketing, thereby integrating consumer-branding messages through carefully planned, strategic co-promotion with trade partners.

This book will study co-marketing as practiced by some forward-thinking manufacturers who have begun to take a different view of co-op advertising and trade marketing. It will investigate strategies to redirect co-op dollars from ambiguous, immeasurable efforts to specific programs that reinforce branding goals. At the same time, there will be an examination of how the fact-based spending model of co-marketing helps to develop better relationships with key trade partners as it helps to grow market share, speed product turn, and increase profitability. There will also be examples in which co-op ads have damaged finely crafted corporate brands. Then the ways in which co-marketing programs coordinate the brand messages conveyed through trade marketing with the messages delivered through consumer marketing will be emphasized. Finally, this book will look at some manufacturers who have created fact-based selling environments to extend the delivery of their corporate marketing strategies.

This book is divided into two parts. Part I reviews the evolution of co-op advertising, retailing, and branding. I liken co-op to an abandoned stepchild, while consumer marketing and branding is the favorite son. I show how trade marketing has grown into a "great cash giveaway" and has become a bone of contention between most manufacturers and their distribution partners. Part I explores the role of information in the balance of power between manufacturer and retailer, and reviews the importance of branding for both manufacturer and retailer. Many examples of both successful co-marketing ventures and failed co-op advertising efforts support the ideas presented. Many of these examples come from my own personal experiences and deliver an insider's look at some important marketing success stories.

Part II introduces the eight-step co-marketing process and its advantages. Many actual co-marketing programs are discussed with an emphasis on the role of information in successful campaigns. Lessons learned from research are explored as well as the value of providing the sales force with the kind of facts that, in the eyes of retailers, transform them from pests into partners. Small-company strategies for employing co-marketing principles are investigated, and, a case is made for elevating co-marketing to brand status.

Part II also presents a step-by-step approach for putting a co-marketing program into practice at your company. The result of rigorous research and mathematical analysis, the eight-step-process Co-Marketing Solution is based on experience gained from reengineering the co-op programs of several major corporations. The second part of the book is replete with examples of both successful co-marketing ventures and failed co-op advertising ventures.

My hope is that you will put co-marketing principles to work in your company and elevate trade marketing to the same status as consumer marketing. In this context, you will learn to appreciate the point of sale (POS) as an important marketing medium, and you will learn to respect the people who control it—the trade—as strategic partners who can profoundly impact the total marketing efforts.

PART 1

The Manufacturer, the Brand, and the Retailer: A Historical Perspective

The first part of this book reviews the evolution of co-op advertising. It chronicles the evolution of co-op, retailing, and brand management. The merit and methods of valuing a brand name are reviewed, and the importance of managing the co-op budget is presented. Co-op and trade marketing are shown to be a multibillion-dollar area that is undermanaged by most U.S. companies.

1

The Great Cash Giveaway

Co-op advertising is simply the way that manufacturers pay for some or all of the costs when retailers advertise their products. Co-op advertising has been around since the early 1900s. No one can say for sure when it really started or what the first co-op venture was. Most likely, it began as a fairly innocent business proposition.

I imagine that once upon a time a retailer told a manufacturer he would like to advertise the manufacturer's product. The retailer suggested it was only fair that the manufacturer share the burden of paying for the advertisements. Both parties probably agreed that to satisfy the demand generated by the advertisements, more of the product would need to be purchased and stocked. Maybe even back-room stock would be required. A little salesman may have appeared on the manufacturer's shoulder to promote the idea, "If you can sell-in a good deal more product through this ad, why not pay part of the advertising? It's almost like a volume discount." A little accountant may have appeared on the manufacturer's other shoulder to warn, "It would be dangerous to give the retailer carte blanche on spending our money." So the manufacturer set a limit on how much of his money the retailer could spend.

An agreement might have been reached in which the manufacturer would share fifty-fifty in the cost of the advertisement, up to a certain point. That point would depend upon purchases of the manufacturer's product by the retailer. A common procedure was to set aside a certain percentage of the product's sales for the retailer to use to promote that product. A figure of 2 percent was commonly used in examples. "Do not front the money to the retailers either," the cautious accountant probably admonished. "And insist on some proof that the ad was indeed run."

This evolution of co-op advertising was fueled by forward-thinking companies like Procter & Gamble, whose management team focused on the fledgling use of consumer advertising and product management to brand their products. If the retailer wanted to feel a part of the action, what harm was there in marking up the price and setting aside a couple of percentage points for retailers to use to buy local market advertising? Thus was created the marketing paradigm where the manufacturer used advertising and promotion to create consumer awareness and demand while the retailer advertised price and availability locally.

Over the years, this seemingly innocuous practice would become the accepted way for manufacturers to appease their retailers. And for their salespeople, co-op would become an important closing tool: "I'll help pay for the advertising if you place this order." For the manufacturers' financial people, co-op dollars would never become an issue. As a variable cost of doing business, these dollars were rarely, if ever, scrutinized. The manufacturers' sales departments promised to provide the co-op dollars to the retailers. Administrators, usually in sales or finance, paid out the funds. But no one really managed these dollars. This dynamic evolved into what has become today's "great cash giveaway."

A Multibillion-Dollar Problem

Payment practices vary greatly from company to company, so it is difficult to pinpoint exactly how much is paid out in co-op dollars. In a 1993 study, ACNielsen estimated that manufacturers allot some

$11 billion a year through various co-op programs. Other estimates have been substantially higher. It is fair to say that $15 billion represents a conservative estimate. Although the exact dollar amount manufacturers spend on co-op programs is not known, it is true that most manufacturers reluctantly participate in co-op and view it—in its present state—as a necessary evil. Generally, manufacturers who sell their products through two- or three-step distribution are forced to participate in the co-op process. The more retail-oriented the product is, the more it is advertised. The more the product is advertised, the more money is spent on co-op.

The percent of sales allocated for co-op advertising, or co-op allowance, varies not only from industry to industry but also from manufacturer to manufacturer within a specific industry. Generally speaking, high-margin products, such as drugs, software, and cosmetics, offer higher co-op allowances. For high-margin products, co-op allowances between 6 and 8 percent of sales are not unusual. On the other hand, low-margin manufacturers, such as computers and textiles, tend to offer lower co-op allowances. For such companies, allowances frequently remain between 1 and 2 percent.

Since many co-op advertising programs are administered in-house, information on program terms and total payout dollars is not readily accessible. Despite lack of precise percentages and dollar figures, it is clear that if co-op is a problem, it is a huge problem. For a major manufacturer in the Fortune 1000, co-op advertising can easily reach a hundred million dollars a year!

Some 60 percent of the marketing budget for a consumer product is spent on trade support. That trade support includes promotional allowances, merchandising, event marketing, and co-op. That means the trade budget is usually larger than the consumer-marketing budget. It makes one wonder what kinds of programs are being used to deliver this amazing amount of budgeted spending and how those programs are being managed.

In 1994, Multi-Ad performed an analysis of published co-op programs. Their analysis included 3,328 programs. About 68 percent (2,257) were handled in-house, and 32 percent (1,071) were handled by outside agencies. Multi-Ad looked at two statistics, the participation percentage, which is the percentage of available funds actually paid (also called the reimbursement percentage), and the accrual percentage, which is the percentage of sales earmarked for funding the co-op. Table 1.1 shows the results.

The numbers published by Multi-Ad point to two irrefutable facts:

1. Co-op is a huge expenditure of potential marketing dollars.
2. The types of programs vary greatly.

In this age of micromanaging the consumer-marketing budget and right-sizing the corporate workforce, it is almost comical that enormous co-op budgets have escaped the attention of marketing and financial managers. The situation evokes a famous quote in the advertising world credited to John Wanamaker: "We know 50 percent of consumer advertising works to build sales, but the problem is we don't know which 50 percent." In the world of co-op advertising, 50 percent knowledge of what works would be a tremendous improvement over today's sorry state of affairs. Few companies have solid data showing how co-op money is being spent. Fewer still study the impact this spending has in driving sales. The systems required to track spending patterns are costly, and most manufacturers haven't seen the reason to invest in them, until now.

Uncertainty over the effectiveness of co-op advertising would prompt most manufacturers to discontinue their co-op programs—if only they could get away with it. But they know they can't with-

TABLE 1.1 Analysis of Published Co-Op Program Terms

Accrual %		Participation %	
1%	10%	50%	37%
2%	31%	75%	2%
3%	23%	100%	23%
4%	5%	<50%	38%
5%	22%		
>5%	7%		

Programs handled in-house: 2,257 (68%)
Programs handled outside: 1,071 (32%)

(Source: Multi-Ad)

Table 1.1 illustrates the different terms of 3,328 co-op advertising programs analyzed by Multi-Ad. It shows amount set aside, percent of sales (accrual), percent paid (participation) by manufacturer, and who administered the program.

out losing significant trade support for their products and distribution. Co-op advertising has evolved into an integral part of the manufacturer-retailer dynamic. Executives today have come to accept co-op advertising as an unpleasant fact of life. The size and potential of these dollars when managed strategically, however, is making some forward-thinking executives sit up and take notice.

Abandoned Stepchild

When it comes to co-op advertising, modern business has found itself in a state of oblivion. An enormous sum of money is spent on co-op advertising and trade promotion each year. Redirected to the bottom line, this sum would easily represent 25 to 50 percent of net profit for most companies. Yet little or no data exists on how the money is being spent, resulting in financial and marketing people being unable to perform a return on investment (ROI) analysis. When it comes to consumer marketing, on the other hand, management has remained on top of everything. Corporate executives know exactly how much is being spent, how it is being spent, and the ROI produced by this expenditure.

The contrast between the treatment of the consumer-marketing budget and the co-op budget is staggering. Consumer marketing is much like the favorite child, sent to the best schools and given loving attention and care. The trade budget, particularly the co-op budget, is much like the abandoned stepchild. Its future is considered bankrupt, and it is regarded as a nuisance—just another mouth to feed.

My own experience buttresses this analogy. In the 14 years I spent managing brand-marketing budgets for four Fortune 500 companies, I was asked thousands of questions about the consumer marketplace and the use of consumer-marketing funds. But I was never asked a single question about co-op and the use of co-op advertising funds. In hindsight, the enormous difference in interest between the two types of market spending is incomprehensible.

As a brand manager, I spent 90 percent of my time in the analysis of market trends looking for signs of market-share growth. I analyzed to the minutest detail the effect of each coupon dropped and each advertising campaign run. I studied the effects of those devices on consumer attitudes, awareness, and purchase decisions. No reasonable expense was spared when it came to generating sell-through and communicating brand messages at the best possible price.

At great expense, audit data (Sales and Marketing Information, Inc. [SAMI] and ACNielsen) were purchased to study warehouse- and retail-level product movement for every market in the country. Hundreds of thousands of dollars were invested with advertising agencies for the development of new advertising themes and the application of these themes as commercials. Tens of millions of dollars were spent on media to deliver the carefully crafted messages to the target consumers. Large sums were spent testing these commercials even before they were aired nationally. Countless test markets were conducted to determine the effects of different product, pricing, or budget mixes. Results of all this research and testing were analyzed and compared to national trends, all in hopes of uncovering opportunities to increase market share.

All in all, big dollars and time were spent on consumer marketing. This market-driven approach can fairly be described as scientific in nature and exhaustive in scope. It was a proven and highly effective way to manage a branded product.

While all this activity went into maximizing the impact of the consumer-marketing budget, the co-op dollars were left unattended—ignored even though their amount was as large as (often larger than) the consumer-marketing budget. In fact, the co-op advertising budget was never mentioned. It didn't even hit the radar screens of corporate strategic thinkers. Co-op advertising truly lived the life of an abandoned stepchild.

Who's in Charge of This Budget Anyway?

Many in corporate America bow with reverential awe to the budget for consumer marketing. Dollars committed to consumer marketing represent discretionary spending—if they are not spent, they go directly to the bottom line as profit. Consumer spending must be justified by quantifying the return or effectiveness of each dollar spent. Make mistakes with these funds and heads will roll.

Executives are far less protective of co-op dollars. In fact, this "top-line" budget simply refers to the difference between gross and net sales. It rarely shows up in any corporate budgets. As a variable cost of sales, it is funny money, only a paper transfer of funds. No one in particular manages it. Few executives have ever been questioned about it.

Legal requirements, however, do restrict how co-op money can be spent. Federal trade regulations, particularly the Robinson-Patman Act, prevent the use of co-op funds in price fixing. Those involved should be familiar with the regulations that pertain to co-op (please refer to *Co-Op Advertising*).

In many cases, co-op dollars are spent by a company's sales department and are used to negotiate the next sale. These dollars are not always put directly into co-advertising or co-promotion of the product. In fact, some may question the basis of this sort of negotiation from a business practice's viewpoint. On more than one occasion, co-op dollars have paid for an important buyer's way to the Super Bowl, a round of golf, or the Final Four. Not infrequently, retailers file claims for advertising they never ran. The funds were diverted to pad the bottom line or, in survival-mode situations, to make payroll.

For most companies, denial is the name of the game when it comes to managing the co-op budget. Of course, there are attempts at management; but since the co-op budget is viewed as a variable cost of sales rather than a cost center, the attempts are not necessarily whole-hearted. The common complaint is the lack of visibility and cost-effectiveness of these funds and the difficulty in tracking how the money is really spent.

Actual co-op dollars are paid by armies of accountant-like clerks—either direct employees of the manufacturer or employees of a third-party vendor representing the manufacturer. These payers employ a variety of validation methods. Some companies audit claims to determine their validity. Some third-party firms even measure ad space and require original invoices to be submitted, so they can check ad prices to verify reasonableness. Some manufacturers become "co-op cops," trying to police the irregularities they find with retailers and wholesalers.

The cop mentality usually has disastrous results. After all, what action can be taken when it is discovered that a large customer has falsified a co-op claim? Punishment leads to bad feelings between manufacturer and retailers, and eventual loss of distribution—a poor prospect at best. Knowledge without action leads to resentment, which ultimately clouds the relationship with the account and can transfer over to how management feels toward all of their trade partners. Sometimes, in a traditional co-op environment, the old adage "what you don't know won't hurt you" can seem the wisest path to take. When attempts to audit fail, companies often just throw up their hands and pay claims as they come in, hoping against hope to keep abuse as low as possible.

At times, auditors uncover provable abuses—even bogus documentation for payment—and are told by the sales department to let it go. The manufacturer may feel a retailer is too powerful to question. Too close of scrutiny may mean a problem getting next month's order or even a possibility of losing that retail outlet altogether.

In the big picture, the salesperson finds he is playing the co-op chip customer by customer. The administrator who pays the claims knows better than to question the situation. The finance department may question the co-op spending policies, but the sales and legal departments may caution the finance department not to look too closely at what's being done, because some of the practices are the necessary evils of doing business.

A recent article in a respected magazine summarized the state of the co-op budget. In their "Survey of Retailing," the editors of *The Economist* noted, "In America, the Robinson-Patman Act requires manufacturers to sell at a single price in a given market, but in practice they give large discounts dressed up as 'promotional money' to big retailers." Promotional money plays a major role in the shifts occurring in today's economy. Retailers have usurped power from manufacturers and are using manufacturers' promotional money to claim their rights to the consumers. Many unsuspecting manufacturers wake up one day to find themselves at the mercy of the retailers.

Some forward-thinking manufacturers, however, are well aware of the shift in the marketing equation and are using this awareness to adjust their marketing strategies to gain advantages over their competitors.

The Marketing Landscape of the 1970s and 1980s

In the 1970s and 1980s, the manufacturer's headquarters controlled the creation of market demand for a product. The national advertising budget was the vehicle used to convey the product message. In some cases, to prompt consumer trial of a product or to repeat business, coupons or product samples were delivered to targeted consumers in select markets. But even in that case, the corporate marketing department was in complete control of the marketing execution. Generating the demand for a product was marketing job number one at corporate headquarters.

During those two decades of corporate control, what was the status of co-op? Co-op was an afterthought. It was a bone that sales personnel could offer the retailer to ensure that sufficient product was available at retail to support expected sales.

Salespeople were armed with information from the marketing department that helped them manage their retail relationships. In the 1970s through the mid-1980s, the manufacturer's salespeople knew more about the retail shelf movement of product than the retailer did. The salesperson was armed with SAMI, data showing how much product was moving out of warehouses to retailers by market. The salesperson also had data from ACNielsen showing how much product was moving off the retail shelves. Finally, the salesperson brought to the table actual shipment data showing what product was sold to which retailer.

The retailer, on the other hand, had no direct access to these data. The retailer was dependent on the salesperson's knowledge. It was the job of the salesperson to educate the retailer and, in the process, procure as much valuable shelf space as possible. As more and more manufacturers began to follow this model, the fight for shelf space was on.

A salesperson might explain to the retailer that a marketing blitz was planned. The blitz might consist of heavy advertising, a coupon drop, a product sampling effort, or a combination. By reaching some 30 to 70 percent of households, the blitz would, the retailer was told, create abnormally heavy demand for the product. The salesperson would request from the retailer extra shelf and display space to stock the additional product required to meet the demand the blitz was supposed to generate. In order to secure the retailer's cooperation, an extra allowance of 5 to 10 percent off the normal case price might be offered.

In the 1970s through the mid-1980s, some manufacturers—Procter & Gamble, Campbell's soup, Unilever, and others—became so adept at working this product push–demand pull formula that they seemed to own the shelves within their product categories. Other companies—R.J. Reynolds and Frito-Lay—guaranteed prime shelf space by giving fixtures to the retailer and having their salespeople stock those fixtures. Much of that shelf space was conveniently located as close to the cash register as possible.

Using these proven formulas, brand managers controlled market demand almost like puppeteers. Retail distribution for a given product simply followed. By the 1970s, many branded products had established followings among American homemakers. Loyal purchasers demanded that retailers carry the established brands seen on TV. Retailers did not want to disappoint or lose customers, so they made sure that the branded products were available in their stores. Manufacturers with strong brands began to exercise incredible leverage over retailers.

Retailers had no choice but to cooperate. If retailers resisted—or, in the manufacturers' opinion, if retailers became too greedy—manufacturers could pull their products. Woe to the retailer who did not stock a major brand like Tide soap when a consumer came for it with coupons in hand. In the two decades prior to the 1990s, the manufacturers with the strongest brands controlled the retail shelves. With no alternatives, retailers had to rely on manufacturers to create consumer demand and to supply sufficient quantities of products.

At that time, co-op played a passive role. The sales department primarily used co-op dollars as little goodies to placate obstinate or shrewd retailers. From the manufacturer's point of view, it made sense for the retailer to run a price-off promotion in the newspaper at the same time the product was being advertised nationally, didn't it? Also, the mission was to ensure that adequate product was in stock at the retail level to meet the market demand being generated. Some very successful brands generated enough consumer demand that the manufacturers could demand shelf space from the retailers without having to pay co-op.

In those days, much of the money allocated to co-op—usually 2 to 5 percent of sales—was never claimed. Sometimes the retailer didn't advertise. Sometimes the rules to obtain co-op funds were so confusing that retailers didn't bother trying to collect. And those who did became so frustrated that they never filed future claims. Retail considerations such as extra shelf and display space were provided at no cost, so there was no reason to put in a claim for them. The retailers trusted the manufacturers, who knew how to create demand for their products.

Over the years, the practice of co-op moved from consumer packaged-goods companies to virtually any manufacturer working through retail. Hard goods like TVs and appliances, soft goods, computers, and clothing manufacturers all began to use co-op to offset part of the cost of their retailer advertising. Life was good for manufacturers, retailers, and their relationship in the 1970s and early 1980s. But it didn't last. By the late 1980s and early 1990s the retail environment changed dramatically. That change was to forever alter the way manufacturers and retailers worked together.

The Changing Retail Environment

The cozy relationship between manufacturer and retailer soured in the 1990s. But to understand why, it is helpful to review the changes retailers faced beginning in the 1960s. The balance of power between manufacturer and retailer ebbed and flowed over the next 40 years.

The 1960s and 1970s were a time of dramatic societal changes. The world of retailing was changing almost as fast. Prior to the 1960s, manufacturers owned the brands retailers wanted. Retailers had something to exchange for those brands. Real estate brokers call that something the three most important determinants of value: location, location, and location. Retailers owned prize city locations, and that's where manufacturers wanted their products.

But times changed. During the 1960s and 1970s, the great inner-city retail locations deteriorated as the urban shoppers with enough money moved to suburbia. The retail merchants followed. Abandoning Main Street, the neighborhood store relocated to the shopping mall.

Soon superstores threatened a variety of neighborhood stores by incorporating all of their goods under one roof. Offering lower prices and convenient "one-stop shopping," the superstores cut sharply into the once-loyal following of the mom-and-pops. The concept of neighborhood shopping lost its meaning. Shopping was no longer a local, retail phenomenon. Furthermore, shopkeepers were no longer part of the community. Corporations now owned outlets and superstores with headquarters in remote places.

With malls and superstores now far from most neighborhoods, shopping became a leisure-time activity. Customers willingly drove out of their neighborhoods to shop at stores featuring lower prices and a larger array of goods. While the malls and superstores meant longer drives, they also meant fewer stops.

Even the small town was not immune to the massive changes sweeping across the American retail scene. Sam Walton and his Wal-Mart stores brought retailing in small-town U.S.A. to a new level. Next in the cycle of retailing tumult came the "category killers," such as Toys "R" Us, Safeway, and Home Depot. Through economies of scale, these chains dominated their categories so thoroughly that competition withered away.

Thus the retail environment underwent nothing short of a revolution. The transition from local retailing to "destination" retailing caused serious upheaval. Superstores sucked customers out of traditional inner-city and neighborhood locations.

As long as both the old stores and the new stores remained in business, a glut of retail shelf space persisted. Not only was there more shelf space than American shoppers needed, but much of it was in the wrong locations.

Local market retailers were hurting. The knee-jerk response of some was to try to compete with the national chains by appealing to customer loyalty and community pride. Not surprisingly, this appeal fell on deaf ears.

Some local retailers knew from the get-go that they couldn't use loyalty to compete, and others—those who were financially able to withstand the initial onslaught—soon came to that realization, too.

For them, honing in on service-oriented customers willing to pay extra—and giving these customers additional perceived value in the form of more personal or better service—was the only path to salvation. Even for those who were able to jump successfully onto the service bandwagon, life was not the same as it was before the revolution.

The superstore front began to mature in the 1990s. With that maturity, low prices became the rallying cry. Stiff price competition meant that both margins and profitability would suffer. Profits reached an incredible low average figure of 1.5 percent in supermarkets. American retailing was in desperate need of a savior.

The savior was information, which rode in on the shoulders of new technology, from scanners to computers. Computer technology provided information systems that could track inventory and point of sale (POS). Computer-read UPC (universal product codes) enabled retailers to collect for themselves the information previously supplied by the manufacturer.

The search for margin also ushered in an increase in private-label products. Store brands helped erode some of the effectiveness of branded products as retailers began to merchandise them as appealingly priced substitutes for national brands. In Europe, stores that used their own label products were able to generate 8 percent net operating profits in food stores. That compared quite favorably to the U.S. figure of less than 2 percent. It didn't take retailers long to realize there was more money in putting their own brands on the shelves rather than some national brands. The focus of retailing shifted from having the right product on the shelf to financial survival. The war between manufacturers and retailers had begun.

Retailers invested in computer technology because it could tell them what product was selling, what rate that product was selling at, and what contribution to profit that product was making. Retailers with computers knew an incredible amount more about the products they sold than did their precomputer predecessors. For the first time, retailers knew more about product movement in their stores than manufacturers did. And they no longer depended upon manufacturers for information about product sale rates.

This shift in knowledge led to a major shift in leverage between manufacturers and retailers. In fact, the category killers were so confident of their power that they turned to the manufacturers to fund part of the cost of their new information systems. Most manufacturers had no choice except to cooperate. The loss of distribution at a Safeway, Home Depot, or Wal-Mart could ruin at least one year of profitability for even the largest U.S. company. The need for American management to continually increase sales and profit to maximize the value of their stocks left little choice but to cooperate with large retailers, who now held most of the leverage.

Next, the category killers began to hire from the same pool of top business school graduates as the manufacturers'. Instead of running brands and product lines for manufacturers, these business schoolers were planning stores and developing category marketing plans for the category killers.

With help from their own consultants and strategists, retailers realized they had more to sell than just product. Manufacturers were willing to pay for store features such as shelf space and display areas. These marketable commodities helped to generate survival revenue. Manufacturers valued displays at the cash register like gold. As this dawned on retailers, they began auctioning off these displays to the highest bidders.

Retailers also found pots of money available from manufacturers for merchandising and advertising. This money could be claimed to help offset costs. Better yet, retailers found that manufacturers did not watch this money very closely. In fact, retailers discovered they could often get this money just by asking the salespeople for it. Co-op was made a profit center in the eyes of many retailers. Soon the profit center grew to include all of trade marketing.

The benign co-op budget, originally established only to offset the cost of retailer advertising, swelled by at least 300 percent. Retailers learned to charge manufacturers for everything from slotting allowances and displays, to temporary price reductions and slow-moving inventory. Retailers found this money especially easy to obtain on those occasions when the salesperson was pushing for a big order. No longer was the co-op budget left primarily untapped. Large retailers became very adept at claiming every dollar available to them and then some!

Simply by asking for these dollars and hiring an administrator to fully understand the different rules and requirements, a retailer could easily bring in an additional 2 to 3 percent of sales. For food retailers, for example, this additional revenue meant doubling their profit margins. To keep the squeeze on manufacturers, retailers could, and did, provide incentives to buyers based on the amount of advertising and merchandising funds they were able to wrangle from manufacturers. Dropped from the ranks of marketing partners, manufacturers were reduced to nothing more than vendors. The retailing community happily treated them as such.

Now that the manufacturers' salespeople no longer served as marketing partners, buyers considered phone calls from salespeople as bothersome. Buyers no longer wanted to spend their time listening to salespeople explain product sell-through and why they should stock more of their products and at what prices. Buyers had their own computers and already knew this information. What they wanted to hear about were allowances that could be used to reduce prices, build margins, and offset advertising expenses—and maybe even put more in the buyer's paycheck.

The Worm Turns

The new situation left salespeople in a bind. They were in the position of having to find extra allowance money just to hold the shelf space they already had. It became a dog-eat-dog environment—if they couldn't come up with the money, their competitors would jump at the chance to add incremental sales.

Salespeople found themselves on the firing line. The loyalty once shared by retailers and manufacturers had vanished. The large amounts of profit both had made in the past also vanished. The manufacturer-retailer relationship sank as quickly as profit margins declined.

Retailers began to view co-op money as an entitlement. Many began to ask for it off-invoice without any proof of performance. "Trust us," they said to the manufacturers, "we know how to market your product for you." They saw the allowance of 2 to 5 percent of sales as their money—money to be used to fund their pressing problems of technology and infrastructure investment. Often, they even saw the allowance as their key to corporate survival. Even with co-op funds, many retailers didn't survive—bankruptcies were routine events.

Many of those in retail had little sympathy for the new plight of manufacturers and their salespeople. During the 1970s through the mid-1980s, manufacturers had become greedy about using their superior information and marketing savvy. Large corporate budgets and voracious appetites for shareholder profits made the manufacturers push the retailers too hard. To meet their greedy goals, manufacturers found it necessary to "load the trade"—to ship more product into retail than consumer demand could justify.

In the short term, designing an effective promotion, lowering the price, or giving an unusually generous discount to the consumer could alleviate the problem of too much product. For a while, these tactics might help a manufacturer steal market share from competitors.

But too often, the tactics didn't work. As more and more manufacturers followed the same tactics to make their short-term sales and profit goals, the retailers were stuck with excess shelf stock and back-room inventory. Frequently the slow-moving inventory took the place of products the retailer could sell. Even when the tactics did work, it was for a limited time. It only delayed the inevitable problem of excess stock, resulting from too wide an employment of short-term consumer incentives.

The indiscriminate use of product loading by some manufacturers had eroded the credibility of most manufacturers with the retailing community. Many retailers felt they were literally being dumped on. These retailers now understood that manufacturers could not be trusted to help in planning sales and inventory levels to meet market demand. They realized manufacturers were dumping product on them that the manufacturers knew wouldn't move off the shelves during the planned promotional period. And when the manufacturers failed to generate demand, the retailers paid the price.

Fueled by mistrust and armed with in-house information, retailers assumed roles formerly played by the manufacturers. Buyers turned to category management, combining must-have brands—those shoppers demanded—with second-tier wanna-be brands. These were brands that lacked the strong consumer franchise and were willing to offer discount pricing to gain their shelf space. Retailers also began to rely on private labels—store brands to augment profit margins.

To the chagrin of many manufacturers' salespeople, buyers adopted the attitude that only a few products were must-have. They viewed the remaining shelf space as up for auction. That space went to products that maximized category profit. Often, those products were not name brands.

The day of retailer-created demand had dawned!

Retailer-Created Demand

Retailers had won control of the shelf space away from manufacturers, thanks to their new high-tech abilities to generate information. Point-of-sale technology told retailers what was selling. Just-in-time inventory management reduced inventory costs. Electronic-data-interchange allowed replacement orders to be placed automatically. Retailers seemed in complete control of almost every important aspect of their business, with the exception of one: the customer.

The question became, "Whose customer is it?" Retailers were surprised to find that, despite their many gains, the customer most often belonged to the manufacturers. Through masterful branding jobs, manufacturers had engendered intense consumer loyalties. The brands that established consumer "share of mind" created franchises that not only withstood the test of time, but also repelled the attacks of competitors, including retailers.

These special brands were rewarded with higher price points and stable market shares—two factors that boost profit margins. Retailers saw these rewards. Not surprisingly, they wanted them for their own. Having already wrested the power of using information from manufacturers, retailers turned their attention to the power of consumer branding.

Retailers, particularly the category killers, realized that having created destination-shopping locations, they had taken an important step in establishing the basis for consumer demand. After all, their customers were driving past competitive retailers on the way to shop at their stores. Could retailers use this pull, along with the same tools manufacturers had used, to create another kind of brand loyalty? If so, retailers would have another way to gain more leverage and create more profits. After all, the brands they chose to promote would be the ones that would produce the greatest return. And the customers would then belong to them, not to the manufacturers!

Retailers began to recognize something manufacturers had known for years. While *customers* buy things, *consumers* use products. This subtle shift in perspective from the general to the specific helped retailers begin to tune in to the personal involvement a user has with a product, a fact successful brand manufacturers understood and exploited for decades. Consumer loyalty is built by appealing to the motivations and aspirations that spur usage of a product in the first place. This ability to identify with what consumers want from a product and how they feel when they are using or buying it is the key to successful branding. Most retailers, however, have trouble thinking this way for long. They want to think in black-and-white terms—of product categories with the products or brands replacement parts that can be substituted at will to maximize profitability. One retailer departed from the norm and employed a true consumer-based product approach to branding, thereby creating a major success story that fed both their sales goals and their corporate marketing strategy. Sears' development of the Circle of Beauty product line illustrates the steps that a retailer must take to create a consumer brand.

Sears and the Circle of Beauty

In the early 1990s, executives at Sears found themselves in deep trouble. Sales and profits had been slipping for some time. Once dependable areas—catalog sales in particular—no longer spurred the profit and growth they once had. Many of the older Sears store locations were no longer desirable. Store merchandising had lost its competitive edge. More and more, Sears was competing on a low-price basis with the same products other retailers carried. Sometimes, lower prices attracted former Sears' customers to other stores. Sometimes, those stores were located closer to home and the customer never returned to Sears.

When it came to image, Sears' executives faced a tougher problem. Successful branding of private lines such as Craftsman tools and Roadhandler shocks gave Sears a masculine image. Customers at Sears, however, tended to be women. This produced a real positioning mismatch.

Fortunately, information technology that kept careful track of customers was in place. A 1994 analysis of stores with cosmetics departments revealed an important disparity. While 1.35 million women purchased apparel at these stores annually, only 350,000 women purchased cosmetics. Sears' executives decided to find a way to get the women who shopped for apparel at Sears to also buy cosmetics at Sears.

Sears formed a joint venture with Pierre Rogers, former president of Lancôme, and Annette Golden, a cosmetics industry consultant and veteran of both Estée Lauder and Revlon. These experts created a "store within a store" to market upscale cosmetics at popular prices.

"Lean staff and low overhead coupled with Sears' vast marketing and distribution resources means that Circle of Beauty can offer attractive price points," explained Rogers. The great resources of Sears included a customer base of 33 million who carry a Sears credit card.

Rogers illustrated the price-value ratio on lipstick. At Circle of Beauty, lipstick sold for $8.50, significantly lower than comparable designer brands at $12.50 to $22.50. Yet, with lower prices, higher returns were still possible—higher than even the 40 percent typical for designer brands at department stores.

For Sears, Circle of Beauty was more than a product launch. As an "exclusive national brand," Circle of Beauty offered Sears the same type of prestige that previously had been limited to upscale department stores.

Circle of Beauty consisted of 600 product SKUs (stock-keeping units) custom-formulated and packaged to Sears' specifications. The line represented a whole new way to merchandise the cosmetics category. Specially designed kiosks and specially molded modular shelving were created to form an organized system that facilitated keeping items in stock while at the same time, encouraged shoppers to browse and try products. Products were displayed on open shelving, without backs, to enable either self-service or assisted-service.

Trained beauty counselors were stationed nearby. These in-store counselors were part of a beauty informational service that included a Circle of Beauty Message Center. Women could call in 24 hours a day and tap into a user-friendly menu of topics ranging from skincare solutions to what was new and hot in the world of fashion.

The "store within a store" was given between 500 and 1,200 square feet, depending upon the mother store's size. Some 450 of 800 Sears stores were retrofitted with Circle of Beauty fixtures as part of a dramatic merchandising shift that the retailer began in 1987, with a renewed emphasis on apparel. Since that time, some 3.5 million square feet of Sears retail space was shifted from hard goods to soft goods.

Circle of Beauty made women an "offer they can't refuse." It offered the quality of department store brands, such as Clinique; the look of Lancôme; and prices just above the mass market for Revlon and L'Oréal. The combination of attributes was determined through research that surveyed the needs and wants of its target group of consumers. That group was composed of women who had already shopped at Sears for cosmetics and apparel. Sears researchers found that these women felt intimidated at upscale department stores, where cosmeticians pressured them into buying high-price products they didn't really want. Yet they couldn't find quality products or customer service at stores such as Kmart and Wal-Mart. Circle of Beauty, therefore, filled their needs.

The Circle of Beauty's assisted self-service concept gave customers as much help as they wanted, but no more. There was no pressure, but there was expert advice if it was desired. Customers had opportunities to sample every product offered. And with the Circle of Beauty Message Center, those who felt intimidated by experts on a face-to-face basis could obtain advice over the phone.

The result was a national brand available exclusively at Sears, a brand that was used to reposition the Sears name among low- and middle-income women. Further, Circle of Beauty was intended to provide an important destination purchase for the cosmetics category. That is, women went to Sears to buy Circle of Beauty, and they also picked up apparel and other fashion products while they were there.

How successful was Circle of Beauty? The line quickly gained more than 20 percent of the cosmetic purchases in Sears, and drove up the retailer's annual overall cosmetics sales to more than $500 million. In any book, that's a tremendous success.

Whose Customer Is It?

The success of Circle of Beauty clearly illustrates the ability retailers have to claim the customer. Since the rewards in sales, margins, and customer loyalty are so compelling, more and more retailers can be expected to follow the lead of Sears, especially in light of the pressures of today's retail landscape. But where does this state of affairs leave manufacturers?

As the marketing battle extends to the retail shelf, manufacturers must learn to partner with retailers. Hard times forced retailers into a paradigm shift—a new understanding of how consumers use products. Now perhaps, manufacturers are due for their own paradigm shift, a new understanding of how retailers sell products. The shelf space available is limited. Necessity is the mother of invention—just ask retailers.

Perceptive manufacturers are realizing that if they want to be part of the product mix, they must help to solve the retailers' problems. Learning to use the co-op budget to strategically partner with the trade in the retail and wholesale channels will be fundamental to the future market success of manufacturers.

The marketing battle is evolving from a fight for a share of the consumer's mind to a fight for space on the retail shelf. That's where the emerging practice of co-marketing comes in. Co-marketing is a strategic-level partnering in which both manufacturers and retailers not only sell more product, but also coordinate their strategic positionings and marketing messages to the end-user.

Forward-thinking manufacturers view co-marketing as a strategic opportunity to extend their national marketing messages to the local community. They understand that co-marketing relationships with key retailers can be used to reinforce brand equity and sell-through. These marketers view the retail shelf as another medium—like print or TV advertising—with which to present the appropriate translation of the brand message. Rather than consider their products as simply sitting on the retail shelves, they view the shelf space as an environment they can manipulate to motivate purchase behavior.

The question then becomes: "How can the manufacturer improve sales and help the retailer at the same time?" Manufacturers who find the answer can, along with their retailer partners, reap rewards that more than justify the investments.

The next chapters will look at some manufacturers who have created new-age relationships that benefit both themselves and selected retail partners. These manufacturers have turned their trade-marketing budgets away from great co-op giveaways and into extensions of their corporate marketing strategies.

For Your Review

It is helpful to know the background and development of co-op advertising. In this chapter, you saw the evolution of co-op advertising, from its seemingly harmless and practical beginnings as an incentive for retailers to stock manufacturers' products to its current status as a multibillion-dollar problem for manufacturers:

- While consumer-marketing budgets receive maximum attention, co-op advertising dollars have been largely overlooked.
- As retailers have become more powerful, manufacturers have lost further control over their co-op budgets.

Is your co-op advertising budget out of control?

During the 1970s and mid-1980s, manufacturers wielded great power over both consumers and retailers. But by the late 1980s and early 1990s, the retailer environment changed greatly, shifting the power of generating consumer demand from manufacturers to retailers.

- Manufacturers were no longer copartners with retailers.
- The relationship between manufacturer and retailer became tenuous.
- Profit margins declined for both.

How are your relationships with your retailers? Have your profit margins been declining?

If your co-op budget is losing control, if your retailers feel entitled to your co-op dollars without accountability, and if profit margins are declining all around, the solution lies in repartnering with your retailers. You need to help the retailers solve their profit problems while at the same time take back control of your co-op budget.

2

The Importance of Branding

Just as changes in today's retail environment are leading to innovative strategies, changes in the retail environment in the early 1900s led to the creation of the first brand. Procter & Gamble was the leading producer of manufactured soap products in those days, but its leadership came under attack as more and more manufacturers entered the soap market. The soap market was growing more and more crowded. Competition exerted its inexorable downward pressure on the price of soap, as it had done on all commodities. Procter & Gamble executives didn't want to lower their prices, but they knew they needed something out of the ordinary to reverse the downward spiral.

The Procter & Gamble executives made a radical decision. They decided to give their soap a name and a "personality" to help it stand out in consumers' minds. They wanted to emphasize that their soap was different from the others. That difference gave consumers a reason to pay more for the Tide brand. If convinced of Tide's superior qualities, consumers would request Tide rather than just "soap" at the store. The first brand name was born.

Procter & Gamble execs believed that the customer loyalty developed by Tide would help insulate it from competition. Procter &

Gamble management learned to do much more than just stamp "Tide" on their boxes of soap. Steps were taken to ensure that consumers were fully aware of Tide's personality, and what the Tide name stood for. To ensure that the brand focus was carefully managed, Procter & Gamble executives invented the product positioning statement (also referred to as the positioning strategy statement), and the brand management system was born.

The positioning statement defines the focus of the brand's personality and how it should be communicated. The brand management system makes use of an individual called a brand manager. The brand manager has the responsibility of managing a collection of products that share a common name or label. The brand manager's responsibilities include every aspect of the brand, from product performance and advertising message to pricing, promotion, and manufacturing.

To support the strategy selected for the brand, all the operating departments of the company report to the brand manager, at least on an informal basis. While the rest of the company may be vertically organized, when it comes to managing a particular brand, the brand manager calls the shots. Responsible for ensuring that the personality of the branded product is observed at every level, the brand manager vests his or her authority in a very specific document, the positioning strategy statement.

Tougher than Dirt

To ensure a brand is managed according to stated corporate strategy, a positioning strategy statement is developed. This document is short, yet inclusive and very precise. It includes the important elements of the marketing strategy, such as price and market target, and is used to govern the activities of those working with that particular brand. The positioning strategy statement is intended to keep all brand messages on target and consistent. Brand managers understand that inconsistent messages confuse consumers, and therefore lose sales. Consumers require a clear-cut reason for buying a product, and the positioning strategy statement lays out that reason.

The positioning strategy statement defines six elements of the marketing strategy:

1. **Goal**—what the brand is trying to achieve in sales, profit, and competitive market share.
2. **Target market**—the consumer group or groups the company thinks are most likely to buy the product. Demographic and psychographic (i.e., personal values and lifestyle characteristics) profiles are identified along with regional and seasonal usage trends. The who, where, and when questions about buying are answered.
3. **Focus of sale**—the primary message that differentiates this brand from its competitors. The focus of sale should be meaningful to the target user in a way that promotes and reinforces his or her decision to buy the product.
4. **Unique selling proposition**—all of the supporting details and backup that the company needs to reinforce for the consumer in order to create a "permission to believe"—making the focus of sale a credible message in the mind of the consumer. These details include the number of years the company has been in business, research results showing product superiority, unique product or ingredient usage, and so on.
5. **Product**—description of product specifications, performance characteristics, packaging, sizes, pricing, and margin.
6. **Mood and tone**—the type of personality and attitude that the brand should convey. Examples of tones include serious, humorous, colorful, or highly effective and superior. IBM, for example, wants its products to assume a blue-pin-striped-suit look and feel, a mood and tone suitable for bankers or professional managers.

When properly constructed, the positioning statement clearly defines what the brand label stands for and how that label should be communicated and managed. Tide is an outstanding example of the successful use of a positioning statement.

The target market for Tide soap was defined as traditional women, ages 25 to 45, with children. These women derived a large part of their psychic reward and value from being good mothers. The Tide mother took great pride in keeping a clean house for her family. Procter & Gamble execs determined that Tide soap was to be always shown in a family context, one in which dirt somehow threatened the order of the household. The problem was dirt; the solution was Tide. Before-and-after presentations were used to provide undeniable proof that Tide could solve even the worst dirt or stain problems.

"Tide is tougher than dirt," bellowed Tide's focus-of-sale statement. This simple, five-word statement clearly directed the original positioning for the oldest, and one of the most successful, brand names. It was used continuously over the years to position the product. Tide was always presented to consumers as if it were a weapon in the war against dirt. With Tide at her side, Mom could win the battle no one else gave her a chance to win.

As the market for soap evolved, Procter & Gamble saw a split between consumer demand and their positioning for Tide. Consumers began asking for soaps that were soft, perfumed, or environmentally safe. These personalities were inconsistent with the personality of Tide, the tough soap for traditional, no-nonsense moms.

Procter & Gamble resisted the temptation to reposition Tide. Instead, the company introduced new soap brands to compete in these new target markets. The company introduced brand names like Ivory Snow, Cheer, and Gain. Like Tide, these brands had their own positioning statements to guide the strategies their brand managers used.

Meanwhile, Tide remained Tide, as tough as ever and faithful to its position. When soap purchasers wanted tough, they could still depend upon reliable Tide.

Branding: The Marketing Battle of the 1960s and 1970s

Procter & Gamble management continued to use brand marketing to create a whole company of products with personalities—brands the American homemaker came to view as allies in her work. These allies helped her clean her house and take care of her family. For some, the brand personalities made the products almost seem like friends.

By the 1960s, to support their growing line of brands, Procter & Gamble became the largest user of advertising. Their media spending was so heavy in daytime TV serials watched by nonworking women that the serials became known as soap operas. In time, the soap advertising budget became so large that Procter & Gamble found it more cost-effective to produce their own soap operas than to merely sponsor them.

Over the years, other manufacturers tried to penetrate the Procter & Gamble market, usually by offering lower prices for comparable goods. But these competitors could not overcome Procter & Gamble's dominance. Procter & Gamble brand managers communicated persuasive reasons for consumers to buy, such as the superior taste of Taster's Choice coffee or the quicker absorbency of Bounty paper towels. There were always large numbers of consumers who believed that Procter & Gamble products uniquely met their lifestyles. No wonder they were willing to pay more for them!

In time, the other manufacturers realized that lower prices were not going to beat Procter & Gamble, so they decided to play the Procter & Gamble game. This decision led to a stampede for branding. Executives far and wide adopted the marketing practices that dominated the consumer packaged-goods category in the 1960s and 1970s. With Tide as their model, brand names proliferated in consumer-oriented, frequently purchased categories. Products such as diapers, soap, cosmetics, shaving needs, bathroom products, drugs, and beverages were quickly branded. When the marketing elements for these products were implemented with Procter & Gamble precision, success almost surely followed.

How could other companies achieve Procter & Gamble–like precision? By hiring graduates of the Procter & Gamble brand-management program. And U.S. businesses tripped over themselves in pursuit of these hot commodities. Manufacturers gobbled them up, and the brand management gospel spread rapidly. As other manufacturers learned what the Procter & Gamble grads offered, they, too, spread the message. Marketing careers were made based on successful branding efforts. I was fortunate to observe firsthand two of the most accomplished Procter & Gamble–type brand gurus: Ron Halliday and J. Robb Bell.

Ron Halliday rose from the bottom rung at Johnson & Johnson, assistant product manager, to division president in just five years.

His incredible rise was based, in part, on his repositioning of Johnson & Johnson Baby Shampoo. Ron foresaw a larger market share if adults were to buy the product. He had noticed that the market for hair products was changing in the 1960s. A shift to natural, soft-looking hair was making the greasy look passé. And, American teens were wearing their hair long—very long.

Of course, Johnson & Johnson could have created new products aimed at this target market. But Ron realized they already had the right product—except the target consumer had been the baby, not the baby boomer. Due to Ron's innovative thinking, Johnson & Johnson began advertising their Johnson & Johnson Baby Shampoo products for adult usage, as appropriate to use every day for taking care of natural, healthy-looking hair. Johnson & Johnson Baby Shampoo sales took off. So did Ron's career.

J. Robb Bell was the youngest advertising director in Procter & Gamble history, reaching that title in just five years. Getting to that top level at Procter & Gamble wasn't easy; the competition was fierce. Procter & Gamble had a reputation for hiring ten of the best and brightest graduates from America's top colleges to train them as brand managers. Before they made that grade, they had to go through a veritable gauntlet of management activity. If they didn't wash out—and most did—they could make brand manager in about five years.

The work on the way wasn't exactly executive-like. These top grads had to spend time in the field working retail shelves. They had to work in remote areas of promotion and budgeting. They had to attend to the finest details and mostly unimportant brand issues. They spent long hours proving they could handle the awesome responsibility of managing a Procter & Gamble brand. Only one in ten made it to the position of brand manager. It took an average of five years.

Successful tenure as brand manager was rewarded by promotion to group brand manager, who managed a group of brand managers and their brands. Then the next step up was advertising director, the keeper of the consumer message.

At Procter & Gamble, the advertising director had almost a sacred responsibility. Remember, just one in ten of the "best and brightest" made it even to the first level of brand manager, and that took about five years. In the same amount of time, Bell made it to advertising director, two levels above brand manager. How did he do it? A look at Bell's career after Procter & Gamble provides insight into his genius.

From Food Service to Consumer Brand: Heinz Ketchup

J. Robb Bell was lured away from Procter & Gamble to the post of marketing director at H.J. Heinz. At that time, Heinz was basically a food service company. They had a few key brands from their experience in the restaurant side of the food service market, but branding for consumers was not their forte.

Heinz Ketchup and Heinz Steak Sauce headed up the brand lineup. But the lineup was as ragtag as that of a neighborhood stickball team, operating as it did under the marketing positioning umbrella called Heinz 57 products. The Heinz strategy had been to manufacture any food product the food service industry wanted to buy. The food service industry wanted soups, so Heinz gave it to them. But when Heinz tried to market its soups through grocery stores, they found they could not compete against the brand strength of Campbell's soups.

In the early 1970s, the most successful Heinz consumer product was their ketchup, successful because consumers had for many years seen the bottle on the tables of their favorite restaurants. The legacy of Heinz Ketchup led to a consumer perception of quality, and earned it a 33 percent market share in grocery stores.

But during the decade of the 1970s, Heinz Ketchup came under attack. Stakes for retail shelf space for ketchup were heating up. Regional manufacturers were taking advantage of the changing retail climate, and grocery stores were evolving into large chains. Heinz Ketchup, like many other established products, was facing a crisis.

Heinz had a problem that gave it a further disadvantage. It was a product problem: All other ketchup manufacturers used a rotary-retort cooking process. This cooked the product from the outside in, holding the raw tomato product in a slurry and rotating it against the side of the kettle, which held the bulk of the heat. This process led to a thinner ketchup product.

Heinz, on the other hand, used aseptic cooking, which cooked the product at a steady temperature throughout the entire batch. The result was a much thicker product than ketchup cooked using rotary-retort cooking. Consumers complained that Heinz Ketchup was too thick, making it difficult to pour from the bottle. Besides, Heinz was more expensive than the other ketchup because the aseptic process was more costly.

Yet Heinz couldn't afford to change to rotary-retort cooking, because the bulk of the cost of manufacturing ketchup lies in the cooking process. Heinz was totally integrated down to the crop level. The tomatoes were prepared and cooked using aseptic cooking equipment from the beginning of the process in the fields to the end of the process in the manufacturing plants.

There seemed to be no way out until J. Robb Bell came along with Procter & Gamble product-branding know-how and the clever idea of turning a perceived liability into an asset. J. Robb Bell and Eric Johnson, another Procter & Gamble marketing man Bell recruited to manage ketchup for him, decided to link the ketchup's well-known thickness with the consumer benefit of rich, restaurant-quality taste. They hired the Leo Burnett Advertising Agency of Chicago to create an advertising campaign to drive home the link between thickness and taste.

Bell's marketing dynamic produced fantastic results. Instead of sinking back into the oblivion of a food service product, Heinz Ketchup doubled its market share over the next five years. Heinz remained the price leader *and* became the shelf leader.

Many remember the advertising campaign 30 years after it first aired. Pop singer Carly Simon sang her hit "Anticipation" as viewers watched Heinz Ketchup inch down the bottle. Another ad portrayed the Heinz Ketchup gunslinger as the slowest in the West. The payoff in the commercials was always that "thicker means richer taste." The brilliant marketing campaign capitalized on the product difference only Heinz could offer.

But what about consumers who complained that the ketchup took too long to pour? Bell instinctively reduced the size of the bottle's opening. Remaining true to the "thicker means richer taste" positioning, Bell refused to compromise. To make the ketchup come out faster (and thereby appear nearly as soupy as the competition) would have contradicted the entire positioning message. If consumers associated slow ketchup with rich-tasting ketchup, then the smaller opening made Heinz taste even richer.

Some thought Robb used consumer trickery. Others thought he used marketing brilliance. In either case, the rush was on to find marketing experts like J. Robb Bell. Manufacturers wanted their own experts to brand their products, maintain or generate profitability, and insulate them from competition. As more and more businesses were exposed to the practice of product branding and the art of market adaptation, the seeds were sown for the emergence of co-marketing.

The Value of a Brand

One of the most difficult questions in brand marketing is a financial one: What is a brand name worth? Although difficult, two factors make it an essential question.

First, a valuable brand has a direct bearing on a company's equity, and management is obligated to provide stockholders with financial statements that accurately reflect their equity.

Second, management needs a basis for making and measuring investment decisions on branding. Marketers often invoke the value of a brand when recommending programs to management. After all, the marketers might reason, the company must maintain the strength of (or invest in the future of) their valuable brand.

There are a number of different techniques used to measure a brand's value, but marketers and financial managers do not agree on which is the most precise technique. Many marketers insist there is no exact way to quantify a brand's value. But that has not stopped financial people from including estimates of that value on balance sheets. Here are a few of the methods used to calculate brand value.

Trademark & Licensing Associates

Trademark & Licensing Associates calculate the amount someone would pay to rent or buy the brand name. Then a 20-year cash-value analysis based upon revenue and license value is created.

Take, for example, Gillette. The company's 1994 sales were $6.1 billion. Gillette is a strong brand and therefore would command a relatively high royalty payment, say, 8 percent. With a sales figure of $6.1 billion, 8 percent yields a potential royalty payment of $480 million in the first year.

The $480 million is then compounded at a rate of 3 percent per year (the estimated net inflation) for 20 years (the expected minimum remaining life of the brand name). This cash flow is then discounted back to the present, using Gillette's average cost of capital, just over 10 percent. The result is that Gillette's brand name is calculated to have a value of $5.1 billion. Some better-known brand names are valued according to this method in Table 2.1.

Market Facts

Market Facts, a Chicago-based market research firm, developed their conversion model to measure the strength of the psychological commitment consumers have to a brand and to create an estimate of value based upon that commitment.

TABLE 2.1 Comparison of Brand Valuations

Brand	Status	Market Value
Health and Beauty Aids		
Gillette	Global	$5.1–5.4 billion
Johnson & Johnson	Global	$11.4–11.8 billion
Estée Lauder	Global	$1.0–1.2 billion
Chanel	Mega	$900 million–1.2 billion
Avon	National	$2.4–2.7 billion
Retailing		
Macy's Federated	National	$2.0–2.2 billion
Sears	Transnational	$5.6–5.8 billion
Benetton	Global	$500–550 million
Harrods	Transnational	$800–900 million
Food and Beverage		
Kellogg's	Global	$3.4–3.8 billion
Nestlé	Mega	$25+ billion
Pringles	Transnational	$300–400 million
Coca-Cola	Mega	$25+ billion
Apparel/Fashion		
Nike	Global	$1.3–1.7 billion
Reebok	Transnational	$600–800 million
Dior	Global	$1.0–1.4 billion

(*Source: Market Facts*)

Table 2.1 shows the relative value of some well-known brand names using the Trademark & Licensing method of comparing value to licensing value.

A consumer's psychological commitment is gauged on:

- satisfaction with the current choice
- the importance of the decision to make that choice and the amount of effort that went into the decision
- attitudes toward alternative choices
- the intensity of ambivalence about the choice

Using questionnaires to measure the commitment that consumers have made and their openness to change, a value for the strength of the bond between consumer and brand is determined. This value allows consumers to be placed into segments based on their individual commitment levels.

Once segmented, analyses can be run. For example, one can look at the committed Coke drinker and find out what he or she thinks about the brand. These thoughts can be compared to those of the less-committed or convertible Coke drinker's thoughts. This type of analysis allows marketers to isolate the key psychological components that influence a consumer's commitment to a brand.

Using the conversion model, consumers can be divided into four segments based on the strength of their commitment to the brand: Entrenched, Average, Shallow, and Convertible. Nonusers can also be divided into four groups: Available, Ambivalent, Weakly Unavailable, and Strongly Unavailable.

A strong indicator of future brand health is the direction and the size of the difference between the Convertible and Available segments. This approach is illustrated in Table 2.2 taken from a Market Facts study of soft drinks conducted in 1991.

The data in Table 2.2 reveals weakness in consumer commitment to Coke and Diet Coke. In these two, the percentage of consumers Available to Switch is less than the percentage who are Convertible.

On the other hand, good growth potential is found for several non-cola drinks such as Orange Crush and 7-Up. This strength is indicated by a fairly large positive difference between available and convertible percentages.

The conversion model was found to be accurate. During the first quarter of 1992, 7-Up showed an increase in shipment volume of 8 percent, and the other brands showed directional strengths and weaknesses as predicted.

TABLE 2.2 Brand Conversion Model

	Coke	Pepsi	Diet Coke	Diet Pepsi	Dr Pepper	7-Up	Sprite	Minute Maid	Orange Crush	Mountain Dew
Users	**40%**	**34%**	**20%**	**16%**	**21%**	**15%**	**14%**	**6%**	**6%**	**7%**
Entrenched	4	4	1	1	3	1	1	0	—	—
Average	21	19	10	9	13	8	6	2	3	4
Shallow	12	9	7	4	4	5	6	3	2	2
Convertible	3	2	2	2	1	1	2	1	1	1
Near-Term Potential	**–1**	**+2**	**–1**	**+1**	**+3**	**+5**	**+4**	**+3**	**+5**	**+2**
Available	2	4	1	3	4	6	6	4	6	3
Ambivalent	9	12	6	7	12	17	15	10	13	10
Weakly Unavailable	11	13	9	11	15	22	20	18	19	16
Strongly Unavailable	38	37	64	63	48	40	45	61	56	64
Non Users	**60%**	**66%**	**80%**	**84%**	**79%**	**85%**	**86%**	**94%**	**94%**	**93%**

(Source: Market Facts, 1991)

Table 2.2 shows the brand conversion research from the soft drink category. This data is used to convert brand strength into an estimate of financial value.

Financial World

Intrabrand, a market consulting firm, developed another way to measure a brand's value. *Financial World* magazine uses this method in its annual valuation of brands. In the *Financial World* valuations, a brand's earnings for a given year are determined. Then, earnings are estimated for an unbranded version of the same product based on category earnings for unbranded products. The difference between the two numbers is the net brand-related profit.

Financial World then applies to this difference a multiple equal to earnings per share to calculate a brand's value. The *Financial World* model judges a brand's strengths on six components: (1) leadership (the brand's ability to influence the market), (2) stability, (3) international scope, (4) the brand's ongoing importance to its industry, (5) the effectiveness of the brand's communications, and (6) the security of the brand's legal title.

Using the *Financial World* model for computer manufacturers in 1996, it was found the value of the Compaq brand was $4 billion, up 40 percent from the previous year. Apple, with all its problems, was valued at $741 million, down 80 percent from the previous year. IBM had a negative value!

Success with IBM–compatible personal computers had catapulted the Compaq brand name to the top. Apple suffered from a decline in operating profits and a price-cut designed to ward off competition. IBM's negative brand value was, according to *Financial World*, the result of having "neglected the general switch to the personal computer."

The *Financial World* model has been criticized for its simplicity. For instance, it seems absurd to predict loyalty to the IBM name solely on recent sales. It is very probable that there is a significant amount of latent loyalty for IBM among previous users who are now using a different computer brand.

Blind Taste Tests

Is there any way to measure the value of a brand and demonstrate once and for all that the investment made in branding has tangible value? An experiment run while I was at Hunt-Wesson showed the value of the Heinz brand name concerning ketchup. The experiment involved blind taste tests. Consumers didn't know which ketchup they were tasting. When asked their preference, half selected the Heinz and half selected the Hunt's. On taste alone, it was dead heat.

The experiment was then repeated allowing consumers to know the brand they were tasting. When they could see the labels, they chose Heinz 70 percent of the time—over twice as often as they chose Hunt. The shift of preference was due solely to the power of the Heinz label. This is the most tangible evidence I have ever seen on the power of a brand name to create a preference and a competitive advantage.

Co-Marketing as an Extension of the Brand Budget

The Control Issue

Why worry about what you can't control? If one were to tailor this saying to the world of marketing, one might say, "Why worry about trade marketing when you can't control it?" Control may partly explain why marketing executives traditionally have spent most of their time on consumer rather than trade marketing.

Executives enjoy slaving over consumer-marketing campaigns, sweating every detail. If something doesn't go as planned, heads will roll. Marketers direct what is said, how it is couched, and where it is presented. They control how much is spent, once management has approved the budget. Those budget approvals follow elaborate presentations in which recommendations are usually supported by reams of market research. Once a decision is made in the corporate suite, the wheels begin turning as planned.

The world of trade marketing is not so clear-cut. About all that can be controlled in trade marketing is how licensed trademarks are displayed and the advertised prices. Otherwise, fighting to control the actions of trade partners is a lost cause. Manufacturers cannot control the messages or the media their retail partners choose. The fact that the manufacturers pay for those ads does not grant their executives one ounce of control.

The trade partner may happily take the manufacturer's money only to display messages that undermine the manufacturer's brand. Willful or inadvertent juxtapositions may make the competitor's product appear to be the better value. Trade partners may create a perception of low value for a brand by offering it at a discount, or for free as will be shown in the Motorola example.

To effectively co-market with trade partners, marketers must forego the control and autonomy of consumer marketing. Instead, marketers must attempt to influence their trade partners. It is important for marketers to view co-op advertising and trade-marketing budget as an extension of their consumer budget and to begin managing it with the same focus.

Failure to Control the Message Undermines Motorola Cellular

Motorola's corporate strategy statement was synonymous with quality. In fact, the company practically invented the quality movement in the United States. Through their six-sigma approach, Motorola executives raised the quality bar to a level previously thought impossible in manufacturing. Before six-sigma, the acceptable rate of defective product was three parts out of each one hundred. Motorola left that standard in the dust when it moved to just 6,810 defects in 1,000,000 opportunities (or 6.8 out of every 1,000).

How did Motorola reach this inaccessible standard? The company concentrated on designing products carefully and managing the entire manufacturing process. Motorola's quality breakthrough resulted in a tenfold reduction in defects in 1989 and a hundredfold reduction by 1991. This translated into savings of $500 million in 1990. When the final goal of six-sigma was realized in 1992, the company had achieved savings of $1 billion!

A semiconductor company at heart, Motorola's business strategy revolves around creating and then manufacturing products that use its semiconductors. The Motorola strategy spawned whole new industries, including pagers and cellular telephones.

The company's telecommunications products required unused frequency bandwidths. These bandwidths were under the control of the Federal Communications Commission (FCC). The government auctioned control of unused bandwidths by geographic area.

The "winners" of these FCC licenses became known as agents. Many agents turned out to be entrepreneurs with little business experience and insufficient capital. They were ill equipped to build the infrastructure necessary to turn the licensing opportunity into a successful enterprise. Motorola executives saw an opportunity and jumped in headfirst, without checking the water's depth. Motorola offered agents the investment financing needed to build the infrastructure and to pay for advertising. Some of this financing comprised co-op advertising funds. Motorola generously offered a 3 to 5 percent accrual of sales for co-op advertising and paid 100 percent of the cost of that advertising when the Motorola name or logo was displayed in the ads. That generosity came back to haunt the company.

On one hand, the company committed hundreds of millions of dollars to fully integrate their manufacturing process around six-sigma, the highest-quality standard in business history. But Motorola executives did not stop there. By designating key vendors as strategic suppliers, Motorola management ensured that the quality management principles were employed at all levels of the manufacturing process. Motorola's quality program revolutionized American manufacturing.

On the other hand, agents in the cellular marketplace were unwittingly sabotaging Motorola's quality message. Using Motorola's co-op money, agents offered Motorola cell phones for free to buyers who made long-term commitments. The "free Motorola flip phone" quickly became the standard consumer-level promotion employed by agents nationwide. These agents also soon found that they could use most of the advertising space—paid for by Motorola—to promote their own identities. The Motorola quality message was hardly ever mentioned.

As the market for cellular phones matured, agents would advertise free Motorola flip phones alongside competitors' phones priced between $250 and $400. Consumers began to associate the Motorola brand name with "cheap," not just in terms of price but in terms of quality, too. This "price-perception value" of Motorola phones contradicted the corporate strategy in which the company was investing millions.

Between 1990 and 1997, Motorola invested over $300 million in advertising and promotion through its co-op program. Most of this spending involved 100 percent reimbursement for newspaper or Yellow Pages ads, requiring only that the Motorola logo be included. Much of this $300 million investment backfired, eroding the corporate image of one of America's finest manufacturers.

After some years, Motorola executives realized the dynamics of their co-op program were undermining its corporate image. They immediately made the necessary changes. The co-op guidelines were altered to align them with the corporate strategy. Agent advertising could carry the free-phone offer only if the manufacturer-suggested retail price (MSRP) of the phone was included in the ad. The value level of the phone was communicated to consumers because the competitor's price was also included.

The Motorola story illustrates that an undermanaged co-op program can cripple even an exceptionally well-managed company. Motorola executives simply fell prey to the all-too-common assumption that co-op programs do not require close monitoring. Once management realized how profoundly co-op advertising influenced consumers' perceptions, they took steps to manage their co-op program more closely. Most manufacturers I've talked with are years behind Motorola in their understanding of this important fact.

Although the exact value of a brand name may be difficult to quantify in dollar amounts, the value of branding and its effect on profit margin and return on assets, as well as its use as a competitive barrier to market entry, is clear. Brand name is an important corporate asset, well worth the investment required to establish and perpetuate it.

The effect of successful branding establishes a basis for viewing the money spent as a measurable long-term investment. This concept of branding as a long-term investment is fundamental to the necessary shift in attitude concerning how management views the co-op advertising and trade-marketing budget.

First, the concept of branding as a long-term investment helps executives view the co-op budget as an extension of the branding efforts being presented through the consumer-marketing budget. Second, realizing that the brand actually has value that can be carried on the balance sheet makes executives want to manage and protect that asset. Therefore, they are more attentive to the messages retailers distribute regarding their brands in co-op advertising efforts. After all, consumers see the retailer-placed advertising and not just the manufacturer-placed ads.

Left unattended, the trade can communicate messages that are detrimental to a brand's image. For example, Motorola management spent tens of millions of dollars supporting cellular phone agents who used the money to advertise free Motorola flip phones with their services. Subsequent research showed this broad-scale free-phone offer undermined the Motorola brand image of quality. After all, if it's free, it can't be too good!

Ironically, Motorola had invested a great amount in quality manufacturing processes. They had invented the movement toward product quality in the United States with their six-sigma approach—an approach that revolutionized American manufacturing in terms of reliability and quality.

The Motorola example offers still another reason why corporate executives need to pay more attention to their co-op ventures. Co-op represents more than just money spent to appease retailers. It is an important part of managing an important asset, the brand and all the consumer-level communication associated with it.

Taking Control of the Retail Message

The process of building a successful co-marketing plan resembles the process of engaging an advertising agency to create consumer messages. The company (client) first must introduce the personality of the product line to its new advertising agency. A positioning strategy statement, as we reviewed earlier, conveys this personality best. Armed with this strategic information, the agency conducts market research and performs a thorough review of the products and services. From all of this work, conclusions are drawn together into one brief document called the creative strategy statement.

The creative strategy statement spells out the essentials of the brand's personality, how to present that personality, and how to reach and communicate with the target consumer. Once the client approves the creative strategy statement, this document governs the creation of everything the consumer will see about the product, at least everything under the influence of the advertising agency. The document determines not only the advertising but also the packaging and promotional material. The creative strategy statement will also serve the brand manager at the client's company. The brand manager will evaluate the agency's recommendations in the context of the statement.

The nearly ubiquitous power of the creative strategy statement focuses the brand message and ensures its consistency. The more closely messages adhere to the statement, the more effectively the brand will be established in the consumer's mind. This is the manufacturer's way of being certain that all money spent on advertising drives home a consistent reason for buying their product.

The irony is that the creative strategy statement is sometimes skirted and the brand's positioning is sabotaged. Is it the work of a vicious competitor, a thoughtless brand manager, or an incompetent agency executive? Frequently the blame falls squarely on top of corporate executives who unknowingly pay for co-op advertising that contradicts the positioning of their own brands.

How can executives treat their consumer advertising so carefully while they treat the larger half of their advertising budget so carelessly? While they hold so many accountable on their ad agency spending, they authorize another group to do as they please. This latter group may pay little or no attention to the carefully developed consumer message. In fact, in most cases they don't even know what the company's advertising strategy is. These renegades are the company's retail partners.

Acting individually and in their own self-interests, retailers and other distribution partners promote a manufacturer's product. The manufacturer underwrites much—or sometimes all—of the cost of executing the many retailers' varied promotional decisions. The manufacturer pays, but the retailers decide—often with no guidelines from the manufacturer—on the messages and the media.

Not all retailer decisions damage the manufacturer's brand. But not all retailer decisions benefit the manufacturer's brand, either. Without guidance, what results are literally thousands of separate test markets. In most cases, the manufacturer has no way of tracking the results of all these tests.

For Your Review

A powerful brand can take a flailing product and make it the price and shelf leader, as J. Robb Bell proved with Heinz Ketchup. You can start to establish a powerful brand by creating a product positioning statement, which defines the elements of the marketing strategy: goal, target market, focus of sale, unique selling proposition, product, and mood and tone.

A brand is a very powerful profit-driving asset for manufacturers, as you saw in the story of Procter & Gamble's Tide product. Knowing how much your brand is worth will allow you to

- see your co-op budget as an extension of your branding efforts in your consumer-marketing budget
- see your brand as an asset worth protecting and managing
- be aware of retailing partners' messages and whether they are upholding or damaging your brand's image

You clearly cannot afford to leave your co-op dollars solely in the hands of your retailing partners. The Motorola story showed that the damage to branding efforts can be devastating.

Are you managing your co-op budget and watching whether your partners are holding to your positioning strategy statement? Or do your retailers autonomously determine how the money is spent? Remember, co-op money is not just for appeasing retailers, it is essential for managing an important asset—your brand and its message.

3

Co-Op Begins to Spread Its Wings

Both co-branding and co-marketing involve partnerships aimed at boosting sales of a product. As the name implies, co-branding involves two manufacturers placing their brands on one product in an attempt to project a desired image to the consumer. When executives at Ford wanted to emphasize the styling of one of their new automobile designs, they entered into a licensing agreement with Eddie Bauer to use its name to brand their top-of-the-line Explorer. This move would convey the image of a fashionable sport utility vehicle that combined style and taste.

Co-branding usually involves a licensing agreement to create double recognition and consumer appeal. Ford paid Eddie Bauer a fee to use its name (it usually is a percentage of sales). License fees range from 3 to 8 percent, so manufacturers must consider co-branding carefully.

While co-branding is a permanent bonding at the product level, co-marketing is a temporary partnering at the strategic level. Co-branding is designed to enhance the image of a product. Co-marketing is undertaken to share the cost of a promotional program. A manufacturer may, for example, enter into a co-marketing agreement with a retailer during the launch of a new product. For a limited time, the retailer may be given exclusive rights to sell the new product. The retailer gains by being the exclusive place for consumers to buy the product, and the manufacturer benefits from having a retailer who will promote the product with drama and excitement.

Procter & Gamble management is leading the way in the brave new world of today's co-marketing. Spots for Pampers diapers and Crest toothpaste have been used to promote lower prices at Kmart. Another Procter & Gamble campaign featured actor Gregory Harrison promoting Head & Shoulders shampoo. He is interrupted by a voice-over directing viewers to Lucky Stores where "you can try it for yourself."

The stage for co-marketing is not always a conventional advertising medium. Executives at Keebler's parent, Dow Brands, use the store as a communications medium. Consumers who purchase Keebler cookies at selected stores receive discounts for theme parks, zoos, and museums. By elevating the point of sale to media status, executives at Keebler employ the retail shelf in their marketing plan.

Co-marketing, then, can be an important tool in building brands. The following examples show how co-op advertising and co-marketing have intersected to create brilliant marketing success stories: Chief Auto Parts' story, in which a sagging brand is given a "brand-new" personality; and the unlikely tale of Intel, which employed a new tactic called co-branding to help it become one of the 90s' most powerful new brands.

Retail Branding: Chief Auto Parts

Having spent 12 years in the packaged goods industry, I wondered whether branding principles would work in other market areas. I had my chance to find out when executives at Southland Corporation in Dallas decided to reposition their newly acquired auto parts chain. They tapped me to perform this repositioning.

Best known for its 7-Eleven stores, Southland Corporation had purchased a well-established chain of auto parts stores. The company combined the 18 Texas locations with the 130 stores left in California.

Corporate decision-makers thought they could fit the auto parts chain into their successful 7-Eleven format of convenience and location. They were wrong. Rather than generating sales of the projected $75 million in the first year following the acquisition, sales sagged to just $46 million. Executives decided to reposition the business or get out of it.

As we studied the problem, I knew there would be no easy answer. The auto parts market was mature. Store locations were set, and many of the stores even sported an old-fashioned look and feel. Category revenue was growing by a meager 2 percent, so growth would have to come at the expense of competitors.

With auto parts outfits competing for the same consumers, the battle narrowed almost exclusively to price. At Chief, major category-loss leaders—oil, spark plugs, antifreeze—were on sale over half the time. These items were priced so low that they actually contributed a net loss, even before overhead costs were added in. Product turn (the number of times inventory dollars are replaced in a year) inched along at 1.4 times compared to the goal of 3 or 4 times. Such slow movement provided little opportunity to return any new investment spending.

Analysis of the problem was then shifted to the profitable items and the customers who bought them. I found that hard parts—starters, alternators, water pumps, carburetors, etc.—accounted for 80 percent of the gross profit dollars contributed from sales. Unfortunately, they accounted for only about 15 percent of sales revenue.

Who was buying these hard parts anyway? Would it be possible to attract a disproportionate amount of these highly profitable users? Research revealed that the major purchasers were "shade-tree mechanics," so named to identify them as weekend mechanics. Without access to a mechanic's garage, these do-it-yourselfers frequently toil beneath a shade tree.

A segmentation analysis revealed that these consumers represented 15 percent of their demographic profile. But we needed to understand what motivated their behavior and how they made automotive purchase decisions. To do this we brought 50 of them into our offices and conducted one-on-one, in-depth interviews.

Perhaps the most important information derived from these interviews went unspoken. The *way* participants answered questions provided the nugget of marketing intelligence upon which we could build our marketing platform. We found that they had the unmet, subliminal need to be told they were intelligent. These "salt of the earth" types routinely spent weekends working on cars for their friends, neighbors, or family members. Although they loved the work, their mechanical talents had never been properly acknowledged. In fact, others had sometimes minimized the importance of their mechanical abilities. One could almost hear the echoes of a mother's exhortation, "Why don't you study harder so you don't have to spend so much time under the hood of that old Chevy?" Careful analysis and research had uncovered the keys to the branding solution: boosting sales of the profitable hard parts by satisfying an unmet need among the consumers who purchased them.

Still, the relatively flat nature of the auto parts business would have to be overcome. Those who work on cars themselves will work on cars, and those who don't like to work on cars won't do so. Market share could come from only one source, the competition.

The push to drive sales of hard parts was accomplished partly by making changes at the store level. Rather than secure the hard parts behind the counters and thereby force customers to seek help, new packaging was created and placed on shelves for customers to find for themselves. This strategy recognized the do-it-yourself nature of the customer as well as his need to be treated as intelligent.

To add more profitable hard parts, store inventory levels were reduced from an eight-week's supply to a two-week's supply. This move freed up enough cash to add more than 3,000 hard parts to meet target consumers' needs. Now shade-tree mechanics were more likely to find the parts they needed on the shelf at Chief. And the parts were merchandised out front so it would be obvious how large the selection actually was.

Internal changes, however, were not enough. Consumers had to be made aware that Chief was serious about meeting their needs. Then they had to be lured into the store. Once there, the changes were likely to keep weekend mechanics coming back. The advertising campaign's positioning statement emerged directly from the consumer interviews: "You're smart enough to do it yourself—and you're smart to shop at Chief." The campaign's psychological premise addressed the weekend mechanic's unmet need to be recognized for his intelligence.

An innovative Los Angeles ad agency helped spread the message in a memorable way. The agency personified the "smart" association by bringing in Don Adams, to reprise his role as Maxwell Smart on the 1960s' TV show *Get Smart*. The popular character served as a bumbling—but very precise and confident—spokesman. Tongue-in-cheek commercials featured Adams, his shoe phone, and a sexy sidekick named Parts Galore. The message was always the same: You will find a vast selection and good prices on hard parts at Chief Auto Parts and "you're smart to do it yourself."

Co-marketing was tapped to help fund this campaign. Manufacturers were enlisted to showcase their products in the advertising that featured Adams. Special promotional events, such as the Summer Vacation Fix-Up or the Protect Your Car for Winter special, helped raise co-op money. Many vendors chose to let Adams showcase their products and advanced special co-op funds to pay their share.

Results of the repositioning were outstanding. Top-of-mind awareness among parts purchasers doubled following a six-week, introductory advertising blitz. Not only were do-it-yourselfers attracted, so were gas station mechanics. Sales doubled the first year to $95 million. Due to the skew to more hard parts, profit margins set category highs.

Seven years later, management completed a leveraged buyout of the chain. By that time, sales topped $500 million and profit margins were the industry's best. An integrated branding model once again solved a very serious business problem. And the use of co-op helped fund the consumer message and provided a way for retailer and manufacturer to co-market together.

The Launch of Intel Inside's Co-Branding Program

Intel was a rather anonymous microprocessor-chip company that had passed the $3 billion sales mark in 1990. Up until that time, corporate strategy had been to develop leading-edge technology and to build products to the specifications of design engineers. A strategy to "out-tech" the competition had proved successful, but management became aware that this type of strategy contained a certain element of risk.

Marketing people know that companies relying solely on technology can be quite vulnerable. With the cost of building an Intel production plant approaching the billion-dollar mark, one miscalculation could shut the company down. As each new product was developed, this Santa Clara, California, firm's fate would be on the line. If consumers decided to pass up the new round of technology and stay with the older, cheaper models, Intel's investment would be shot.

Intel may have been a darling of Wall Street, but its executives knew that one stumble could turn it into a dog. They decided on an aggressive end-play to encourage computer manufacturers to buy their chips: They would reach out directly to the consumer to generate demand for the Intel brand.

One of the greatest promotions of all time began in 1991. Intel offered to pay a portion of the advertising cost for the manufacturers using their chips if they would feature the Intel Inside logo in their ads and on their computers. Intel executives knew what they wanted to happen, but no one really knew what to expect. After all, this was the first time executives at a computer parts manufacturer had ever thought to launch a co-op advertising campaign.

The original projection for the program estimated that a total of 50 original equipment manufacturers would enroll in the program. Instead, during the first year, some 1,600 manufacturers, system integrators, and value-added resellers enrolled. The Intel logo appeared so frequently on computer-related advertising that in just 18 months, Intel developed the same amount of brand awareness as NutraSweet did in 18 years!

The bad news: Intel greatly exceeded its co-op budget. The good news: co-op spending was capped at a percentage of sales. The more the co-op budget was exceeded, the more sales rose and the more money Intel made.

During the next few years, Intel effectively used the program to support the introductions of its 286, 386, and 486 chip sets. The program was expanded to include retail accounts with an unusually user-friendly co-op program. Administered by TradeOne Marketing, Intel's third-party processing firm, ads were scanned and those that featured the Intel Inside logo were automatically paid for. For certain classes of trade, it wasn't necessary to file a claim in order to get paid. A check arrived in the mail for those retailers who supported the Intel Inside message in their ads.

Using the program, Intel built tremendous goodwill and loyalty among its trade partners. And in the mind of the consumer, the Intel Inside sticker meant quality. Had Intel succeeded in getting consumers to demand that the computers they bought contained Intel chips? The answer was a resounding "yes." IBM and Compaq, two computer giants, found out the hard way.

IBM and Compaq Test Intel's Mettle

Executives at IBM and Compaq coveted the market position of quality, but their research showed that the Intel name had a lock on it. This research was especially troubling because the personal computer industry was showing signs of acting as a commodity rather than a branded marketplace. In an attempt to shine the spotlight on the quality of their own products, both companies decided to pull out of the Intel Inside program. They continued to buy and use Intel chips, but at the same time, they looked for ways to reduce their reliance on Intel.

The two giants pulled out of the Intel Inside program in the Christmas season of 1994, a time that was shaping up as a bonanza for home computer buyers. It appeared to be an opportune time to test Intel's strength. Other chip manufacturers were producing 486-comparable chips that competed well with Intel's 486. Since the 486 chip was fast enough to run the new multimedia computers featuring CD-ROM technology, most users weren't clamoring for faster chips. The 486-based machines loaded with software were priced in the desirable $1,300 to $1,700 range.

To make matters worse for Intel, a problem with their 486 chip was discovered. Mathematical calculations using the Intel chip produced errors in the fourth decimal place. The popular press coverage had a field day with the story, and Intel suffered a jolt to its image of quality.

As their leadership in the microchip industry hung in the balance, Intel executives saw their worst nightmares materializing.

Demand for faster chips had subsided briefly, handicapping Intel's usual advantage in technology. Its top-of-the-line product for home computers was flawed. And now two leading manufacturers had stopped using the Intel Inside campaign.

What did Intel executives do? They introduced a new chip, the Pentium. But company executives knew that manufacturers wouldn't queue up to buy the new chip. Consumers were happy with the 486, and manufacturers and retailers were set to make plenty of money with it.

Upon the introduction of the Pentium, Intel management informed manufacturers and retailers that all advertising under the Intel Inside program would be restricted to the Pentium. Advertising in support of the Intel 486 would no longer be paid for. Again, Intel appealed to the consumers who wanted to buy computers with Intel. Again, the results were astonishing. Sales of the Pentium soared.

To understand why Intel succeeded against the tide of bad news, it's necessary to flash back to 1993. That year, Intel began running corporate-consumer advertising. Not only did this image advertising complement the co-op efforts, it reinforced the growing perception that the Intel chip was the real computer inside the box. This branding message was brilliantly extended for the Christmas 1994 season.

That Christmas, consumers responded to the Pentium advertising blitz—paid for in part by Intel—that flooded TV and radio. The limited number of higher-priced Pentium-based machines quickly sold out. Consumers who couldn't find one decided that instead of buying a 486, they would wait until a Pentium became available.

By the following summer, the battle was virtually over. Intel had surpassed $17 billion in sales by the end of 1995. Net operating income was an astonishing $3 billion. The public relations problem of the 486 decimal error—in fact the entire 486 chip—was forgotten. Intel had successfully moved the market to a new level of chip performance that they dominated. The Pentium had become the industry standard.

Intel: The Most Profitable Company in History?

Intel executives had learned to use co-branding to drive an entire industry that was restructuring business around the world. Harvard University Professor Emeritus Alfred Chandler predicted in a *Wall*

Street Journal article ("A Chip Giant's Rise," June 7, 1995) that Intel would become the most profitable company in history. "Intel has turned the spiraling cost of competition into a weapon," Chandler said. "That is where the great fortunes have always come from, with economies of scale. No one can compete because the barriers to entry are there. That's what Ford did, what Rockefeller did, and what Carnegie did. It is totally plausible that Intel will become the most profitable company in business history." How did Intel become the subject of such an awesome prediction?

Co-op advertising strategically used to communicate and position the brand name played a lead role. The Intel story serves as a model for the power of co-op and local market advertising. For three years, Intel executives built their brand message and awareness solely through the use of co-op advertising. After three years, Intel corporate began advertising directly to consumers on TV and in print, to complement the co-op branding effort. The message was always the same: "Intel. The computer within."

Intel's emergence as the market leader in the newest and most important manufacturing marketplace in the world attests to the company's technological leadership, but it also attests to its marketing prowess. This "one-two punch" of technology and marketing in modern business history is Intel's legacy.

Intel executives didn't just implement a co-op program; they executed an entire co-marketing strategy. With every passing year, the momentum grew. Initially, the program to partner with manufacturers simply increased brand awareness, thereby reducing Intel's risk when investing in new manufacturing facilities. Within three years, a world-class brand was born that drove sales to record highs. Faced with dire circumstances in 1994, Intel's introduction of the Pentium chip saw sales skyrocket to dizzying heights. The integrated, strategic approach to co-op advertising produced results that exceeded executive expectations every time.

In fact, the co-op program had become so fundamental to the execution of Intel's corporate strategy that executives determined it must be brought in-house. They felt it was a liability for any outside organization, no matter how trustworthy, to have advanced knowledge of the company's co-op plans. For the next two years, TradeOne Marketing assisted in the development and programming of Intel's internal system.

By 1996, the final verdict was in. Intel posted sales of $20.8 billion for the year. The net income was a staggering 25 percent of that amount. Professor Chandler's prediction had become a reality. Intel was well on its way to becoming the most profitable company in business history. Compaq and IBM returned to the program, acknowledging that the presence of the Intel name on their products was an important expression of product quality to their end users.

The Intel Inside program had become the largest co-op advertising program in history, paying out over $300 million a year. Intel's consumer advertising augmented this program. Intel executives introduced their latest product, the MMX chip set during the 1997 Super Bowl. This advertising slot, reserved for the country's top advertisers, cemented the company's place among the who's who of advertising.

The second part of this book will document the advantage that an integrated marketing approach can yield marketers willing to reevaluate their approach to trade marketing. Particular attention is paid to capturing data to measure results, including ROI analysis revealing marketing intelligence that leads to improved sell-through and delivery of brand positioning.

Intel's pioneering co-op program influenced more than just sales of computer chips. It jump-started the evolution of co-op advertising programs from a reactive tactic to a proactive strategy.

The Impact of Intel's Co-Op Program

Perhaps the most startling aspect of the Intel story is the way company executives focused on the co-op program and integrated it into every aspect of their marketing strategy. As the Intel Inside co-op program grew in importance, Intel executives placed more and more emphasis on the marketing data the program could generate. New types of analysis evolved to meet the executives' demands. In fact, it was these many and varied requests that prompted TradeOne Marketing to seek my services in the first place. Intel didn't need help from someone experienced in co-op administration; they needed help from someone with a background in brand management, technology marketing, and marketing strategy.

Through my work with TradeOne Marketing, I saw firsthand the power of Intel's strategic marketing focus. Extensive analyses of program dynamics were made on a continuous basis, sometimes by myself. A veritable army of administrators and marketing managers worked on the co-op program to determine how participants were spending their money—and which activities were yielding the best results in the marketplace. This was the type of analysis I was accustomed to performing as a brand manager in consumer advertising, but never had I been asked to perform such work on behalf of a co-op advertising project.

As I began to work with Intel, my eyes were opened to this opportunity for any manufacturer who took a proactive, market-driven approach to managing their co-op budget. While Intel began to take its sensitive co-op program in-house, my attention turned to other TradeOne Marketing clients who were searching for better ways to manage their co-op funds. In doing so, I continued to adapt the processes used in packaged-goods marketing to the world of co-op.

I found that manufacturers were willing to fund fledgling research projects in areas of attitude and awareness, to find out how their programs were perceived in the marketplace. These manufacturers were willing to pay:

- for quartile analyses to profile how co-op funds were used by various retail or customer segments (e.g., fast growing versus slow growing)
- to have their claims audited for ad content and size to determine how copy points correlated to sales growth
- for sales-force studies to determine retailer issues and implementation needs—studies that sometimes resulted in training programs for salespeople and for customers

In short, these farsighted companies were willing to invest in co-op programs.

It was during this time that my colleagues at TradeOne Marketing and I developed the Co-Marketing Solution. The Co-Marketing Solution integrates the planning, design, administration, and continuous improvement of a co-op trade-marketing program. During these three years, we conducted studies, analyzed data, and planned programs for the likes of Rubbermaid, Octel, GTE, 3M, Sealy, Motorola, and, of course, Intel. This work provided the perfect environment to develop and demonstrate the effectiveness of a focused approach to co-op advertising and the trade-market budget in its entirety.

For Your Review

After having read the success story of Chief Auto Parts, review the activity of your buyers:

- Which buyers are establishing integrated brand models? These channel partners will be proactive in selling your product.
- Are you supporting these channel partners with the co-op funds they need? By doing so, you will create a win-win situation: their strong retailer images will draw more consumers and therefore, sell more of your product.

The Intel Inside story offers good insights on how to proactively use your co-op advertising to lead your product to success:

- Use co-op advertising to build your brand message and awareness. Partnering with other manufacturers and retailers by co-branding helps establish your name.
- Build brand loyalty directly with the consumers. Consumers should not only want the co-branded end product, but should also value that your product is part of the end product.
- Establish your co-op program to reward your channel partners who include your branded product in their advertising. Make sure it is a simple process for them to acquire their co-op dollars.
- It is possible to bounce back from a blow to your image due to a flaw in your product or service. Reestablish your product—for example, Intel's new Pentium chip—and restrict your co-op dollars to those who support your new product.

Let your co-op program spread its wings!

4

A Strategic Approach

In the Motorola story, you saw the downside of allowing co-op programs to run on autopilot. In the Intel story, you saw the upside of managing co-op programs like corporate-consumer marketing campaigns. Indeed, these two case studies clearly indicate that management of co-op programs can have a significant impact on corporate brands.

How can executives ensure that their co-op program is having a positive impact on corporate strategy? Start with a positioning strategy statement. This is the same statement that manufacturers use to build a marketing plan and to manage their brand's personality in the consumer arena. This is the first step in using consumer-marketing principles in the trade-marketing arena.

The Co-Marketing Solution was developed to integrate the design, administration, and continuous improvement of the trade budget. Beginning with an analysis of corporate goals and objectives, the Co-Marketing Solution includes branding and consumer-marketing goals as contained in the positioning strategy statement.

From the positioning statement, a co-marketing plan is developed. This plan directs the co-op advertising program as well as other trade programs such as incentives and rebates. By integrating the co-op venture with other parts of the marketing plan, the Co-Marketing Solution promises to:

- Tailor promotional allowance programs to the different needs of each channel partner in mind. Rather than a one-size-fits-all program, the Co-Marketing Solution recognizes the uniqueness of each type of channel partner and their role in the distribution channel.
- Identify and address the needs of each target segment. Target segments are comprised of homogeneous distribution partners (e.g., large national accounts, distributors, mass merchants, medium-sized accounts, and small accounts). Each of these groups of channel partners may have very different needs and opportunities.
- Provide promotional allowance programs designed with the different needs of each target channel partner in mind.
- Implement each program with precise attention to detail in order to deliver the highest level of customer satisfaction possible.
- Track how funds are spent and measure the impact of those expenditures on customer satisfaction, retail sales, and market share.
- Analyze the relative effectiveness of each promotional event and the ROI for the money spent.
- Adjust the co-op program based on the data gathered. In this way, the Co-Marketing Solution continually improves the effectiveness of the way funds are paid to and spent by channel partners.

The Co-Marketing Solution promotes integration of the myriad aspects of co-op advertising with the rest of the trade marketing effort.

A Better Way to Do It

Similar to the way a new product is developed and launched, the use of the Co-Marketing Solution involves a series of strategic and operating plans. These are devised and implemented to yield measurable data and marketing intelligence.

The Co-Marketing Solution involves

- The development of a co-marketing plan that treats the co-op experience with the magnitude of respect that amount of spending deserves. This plan is similar in development and scope to the consumer-marketing plan, but it focuses on the trade environment. To distill pure marketing intelligence, it is necessary to include data-capture hooks with the initial design of the program. By developing the plan with these hooks in mind, results can be evaluated and a fact-based environment can be created to manage the selling process.

- The development of an administration plan to ensure that customers are treated well and communicated with accurately and frequently.

- The use of data captured in an analytical plan to yield program feedback.

The Co-Marketing Solution encompasses all areas of spending directed at the trade. This, then, means a far greater amount than just the co-op advertising budget. In a previous chapter, the annual cost of co-op advertising was put at a figure of at least $11 billion per year. When other trade budgets—such as sales incentives, product literature, slotting allowances, and market development funds—are included, the total spending is more like $40 billion! These other trade budgets are incorporated within the Co-Marketing Solution.

By carefully planning the program and funneling all activity through a central payment and tracking source, it is possible to focus trade activities on strategic goals and to evaluate the effectiveness of these activities.

When properly applied, the Co-Marketing Solution provides a method to

- effectively integrate corporate strategies and coordinate marketing communication
- measure and enhance levels of customer satisfaction
- gather marketing intelligence to assist in decision making
- develop ROI analysis of trade spending
- develop profit-by-account information

The Co-Marketing Solution uses an eight-step process to plan, launch, pay, and evaluate the effectiveness of trade spending. A real-time, fact-based, continuous improvement cycle is thus created. Figure 4.1 illustrates the high-level steps involved in the Co-Marketing Solution.

By moving through carefully designed steps of planning, implementation, and evaluations, the Co-Marketing Solution aligns corporate strategies and measures their effectiveness throughout the trade marketplace.

From an implementation viewpoint, the development of the specific plans and tactical programs involves the following progression of eight steps:

1. **Identify corporate goals and strategies**.
   Corporate goals are identified, and strategies are set for the eventual translation of these goals into appropriate trade-marketing goals.
2. **Use market research to "bench-mark" the trade environment.**
   The current program is analyzed, researched, and "bench-marked" to determine what current spending patterns are achieving from the participants' points of view, and measure the impact of competitive programs.
3. **Align strategies and define trade-marketing goals.**
   Trade-marketing strategies and programs designed to be in concert with corporate goals are isolated; so is a plan to measure program effectiveness.
4. **Construct the trade-marketing plan.**
   Strategies are developed along with the appropriate tactical plans to implement those strategies, given the needs of each channel and type of account.
5. **Launch the co-marketing plan.**
   The new program—including the very important steps of participant communication and sales-force training—is implemented.

FIGURE 4.1 The Eight Steps of the Co-Marketing Solution

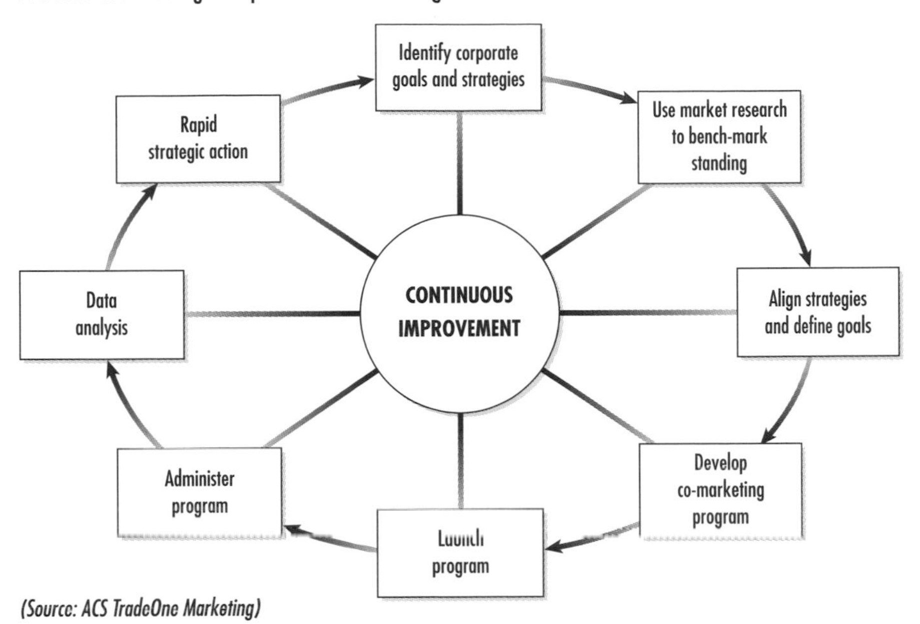

(Source: ACS TradeOne Marketing)

6. **Administer the program and capture data.**
   A plan is developed to set in place the infrastructure required to implement the program. This infrastructure development includes programming the database, hiring and training personnel to deliver customer service, and developing the operating plans and policy manuals for plan administration. The goal is to deliver high levels of satisfaction to customers and salespeople who use the program.
7. **Analyze the data for market intelligence.**
   Activity-usage trends and results among program participants are analyzed to yield marketing intelligence.
8. **Fact-based, continuous improvement.**
   In this post-analysis phase, factual data are used for program revisions that improve the effectiveness and ROI of the trade-market spending.

The Power of an Integrated Solution

When all the elements of the trade-marketing budget are funneled through a central database, it is possible to

- track and report information that tells a very accurate story regarding account performance
- coordinate activity and spending by account
- evaluate account profitability
- calculate ROI of promotional spending

It is possible to summarize this type of information on an account basis and use it to work with the account. Figure 4.2 illustrates a top account profile report that is very helpful for use during regularly scheduled account reviews.

It is also possible to develop reports like the promotion effectiveness report in Table 4.1, which shows the relative cost of moving an incremental unit of goods across the promotions executed in a specific account over the course of the year. This type of analysis is very helpful when working with a buyer to plan the most effective promotions to increase category volume.

When all the data resides in one central source, the opportunities to gain a clearer picture emerge. It's amazing how most businesses lose track of their overall spending because so much of it is handled piecemeal. The ability to track all of the spending including freight, product returns, sales materials, and co-op and promotional spending solves this problem.

Co-marketing also helps reestablish credibility with the retailer. A joint promotion using shared resources guarantees the manufacturer that the retailer "buys into" the program. This means the retailer will stock sufficient extra product to satisfy the expected demand generated by the promotion. The retailer buys into the program because their store isn't just mentioned in the ad, their store is a major part of the consumer message communicated in the ad.

In the absence of a co-marketing approach, a manufacturer might request more shelf space when running a national ad, but find the retailer hesitant. "Without a tie-in for our chain at the end of the spot, I am not convinced your advertising will generate demand for the product in our stores," the buyer might say.

FIGURE 4.2 Top Account Profile (T.A.P.) Report

Account: Retailer 1
Period: Quarter 1, 1999

CO-OP PROGRAM REVIEW

	QTR 1–98	QTR 1–99	% Change
Shipments	$2,750,000	$3,950,000	44%
Accrual	137,500	197,500	44%
Spent	105,000	175,000	67%
TV	5,000	6,500	30%
Print	85,000	155,000	82%
Radio	2,500	4,500	80%
Other	12,500	9,000	–28%
Sell-through	2,520,000	3,923,000	56%

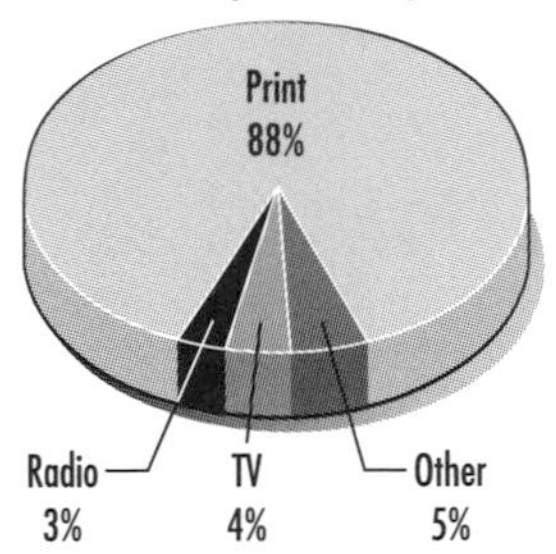

- Shipments up 44 percent, sales up 56 percent
- Print advertising continued as #1 vehicle, increasing 82 percent, likely contributor to increase in sell-through

COMPETITIVE REVIEW—PRINT ADVERTISING

Account Percent of Category Ad Spending = 24%

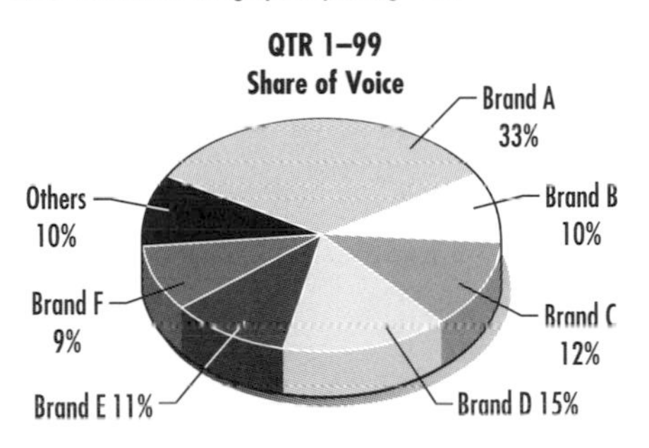

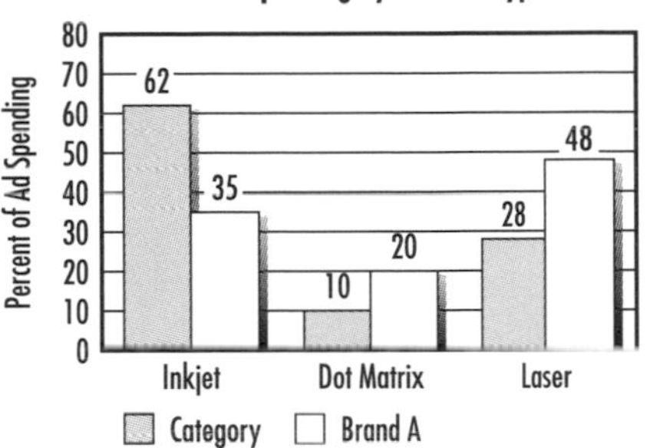

	SHARE OF TOTAL AD DOLLARS		AVERAGE AD SIZE		SHARE OF SEGMENT AD DOLLARS		
	QTR 1–98	QTR 1–99	QTR 1–98	QTR 1–99	Inkjet	QTR 1–98	QTR 1–99
Brand A	22.0%	33.0%	3.5	3.9	45.7%	14.8%	40.2%
Brand B	8.0%	10.0%	2.0	2.5	15.0%	7.7%	10.2%
Brand C	9.0%	12.0%	3.0	3.5	NA	28.3%	0.0%
Brand D	20.0%	15.0%	1.8	1.8	0.0%	0.0%	22.9%
Brand E	6.0%	11.0%	2.5	2.0	39.4%	19.8%	2.7%
Brand F	9.0%	9.0%	2.0	2.0	NA	14.0%	0.0%
Others	26.0%	10.0%	1.5	1.5	0.0%	15.4%	24.0%

- Brand A received the most print dollars at Retailer 1 in the quarter, up 11 share points over last year
- Account also shifted more ad dollars to Brands B, C, and E
- Brand A continued to get the largest ads from accounts, with average size of 3.9
- Brand A's inkjet ad spending is underdeveloped compared to the category (35 percent vs. 62 percent respectively)
- Brand C received the strongest support in dot matrix printers (14 points higher than Brand A)
- Brand A placed strong emphasis on laser printers, while category skewed toward inkjets

(Source: ACS TradeOne Marketing)

Figure 4.2 shows a top account profile report summarizing promotional activity and effectiveness for a key account.

TABLE 4.1 Key Account Promotion Effectiveness Report

Retailer: Quarterly Analysis of the Effectiveness of Ad Support

Promotion	Promo Period	Ad Size	Advertised Price	Estimated Total Ad Cost	Incremental Units Sold	Incremental Revenue–1	Incremental Gross Margin–2	ROI—Promotion Effectiveness–3
Jean Co. Men's Jeans								
Unspecified	3/24/96	6.3	$15.88	$7,938	17,074	$271,135	$86,763	$10.93
Regular/Relaxed/ Stretch Fit	4/21/96	6	17.99	7,560	5,040	90,670	29,014	3.84
Unspecified	5/8/96	0.5	20.99	630	1,252	26,279	8,409	13.35
Unspecified	5/19/96	4	17.99	5,040	670	12,053	3,857	0.77
Jean Co. Men's Shorts								
Unspecified	3/17/96	1	11.99	5,040	1,188	14,244	4,558	0.90
Unspecified	4/21/96	6	11.99	7,560	12,347	148,041	47,373	6.27
Unspecified	5/8/96	0.5	16.09	630	(974)	(15,672)	(5,015)	(8)
Relaxed Fit	5/19/96	4	11.99	5,040	17,383	208,422	66,695	13.23
Relaxed Fit	6/9/96	4.5	10.99	5,670	27,846	306,028	97,929	17.27
Jean Co. Women's Jeans								
Unspecified	3/17/96	3	14.99	3,780	1,465	21,960	7,027	1.87
Unspecified	3/24/96	3	13.88	3,780	2,324	32,257	10,322	2.73
Jean Co. Jr. Boy's Jeans								
Relaxed Fit	3/31/96	5	9.99	6,300	3,117	31,139	4,982	0.79

1– Incremental Revenue = Cost per unit multiplied by the number of incremental units
2–Incremental Gross Margin = Average margin per unit multiplied by the number of incremental units
3–ROI = Incremental Gross Margin divided by ad cost

Table 4.1 is an example of promotion effectiveness and ROI analysis possible on an account-by-account basis.

In the past, manufacturers would push extra product into the stores either by touting the drawing powers of their national promotions or by loading the trade. Manufacturers—especially those who relied heavily on loading the trade—frequently lost their credibility. Retailers would refuse to bring in incremental product despite evidence of large advertising pushes. When those promotions were successful, retailers predictably ran out of product, resulting in an out-of-stock condition.

Today, with computers automatically placing orders based on replenishment stock levels, successful promotions almost guarantee out-of-stock conditions at retail—unless the retailer buys into the promotion and brings extra stock into the store. Co-marketing creates this shared belief in the demand-generation process.

By distilling the spending patterns and types of advertising used by fast-growth accounts, marketers possess intelligence that can boost sales for other accounts. Figure 4.3 is a sales growth profile for Motorola cellular phones performed many years ago when retailers merchandised cell phones primarily by giving them away (e.g., the one-cent flip phone).

FIGURE 4.3 Sales Growth Profiling Expenditure by Product

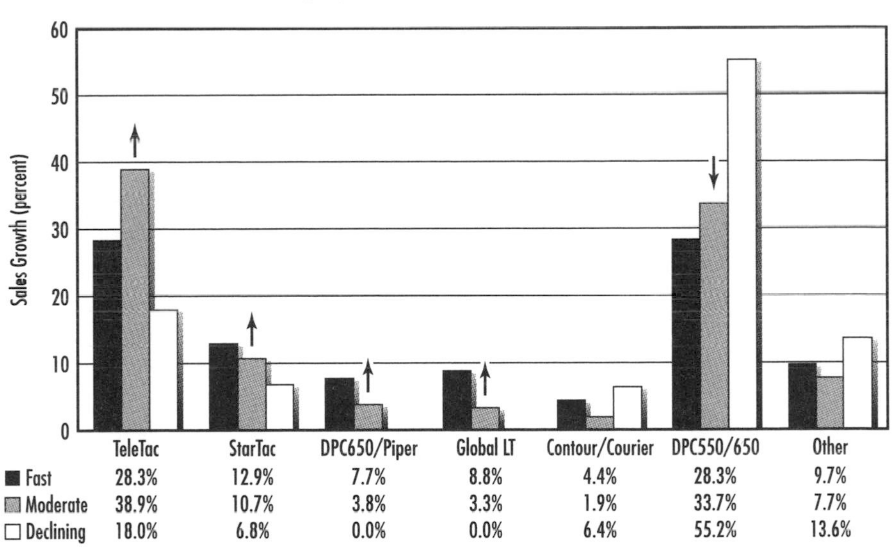

(Source: ACS TradeOne Marketing)

With a retail price of $250 per phone, the cell phone giveaways were an expensive promotion for service providers. The retailers—and Motorola—found themselves in an unfortunate situation. The sales growth profile analysis helped executives resolve the situation.

In Figure 4.4, the first set of bars under each product indicates the fast-growth dealers. The second bar shows the average-growth dealers, and the third bar shows the slow-growth dealers. In this case, the slow-growth dealers weren't growing at all. In fact, their sales were actually declining.

The sales growth profile analysis clearly revealed that the faster-growing retailers were promoting the high-end Startac phone. This phone, which retailed for close to $1,000, was at the time the lightest, smallest cellular phone made and featured a long-lasting lithium battery.

Once retailers were made aware that promoting the Startac model could generate consumer demand—and enhance profit margins—they jumped on the bandwagon. This insight proved to be one of Motorola's most important and successful marketing communications. Both Motorola and the retailers profited handsomely.

FIGURE 4.4 Sales Growth Profiling Ad Features

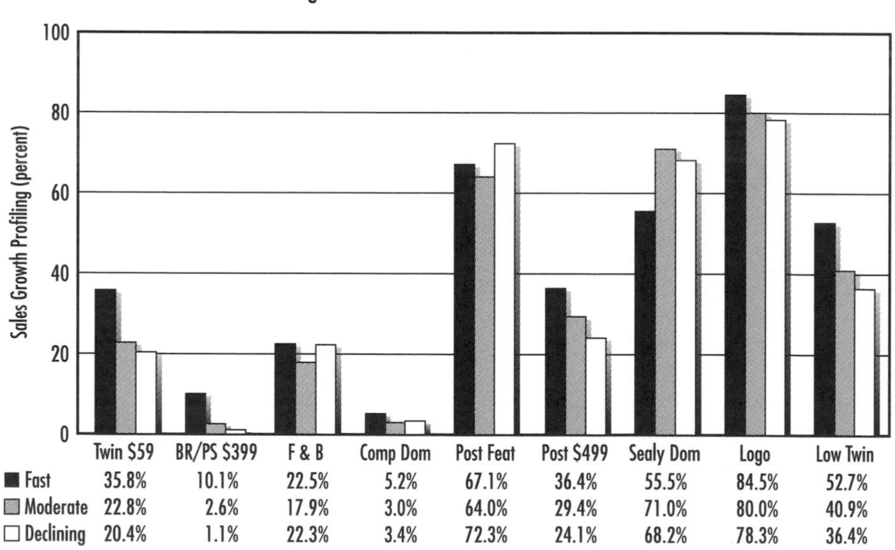

	Twin $59	BR/PS $399	F & B	Comp Dom	Post Feat	Post $499	Sealy Dom	Logo	Low Twin
■ Fast	35.8%	10.1%	22.5%	5.2%	67.1%	36.4%	55.5%	84.5%	52.7%
▩ Moderate	22.8%	2.6%	17.9%	3.0%	64.0%	29.4%	71.0%	80.0%	40.9%
□ Declining	20.4%	1.1%	22.3%	3.4%	72.3%	24.1%	68.2%	78.3%	36.4%

(Source: ACS TradeOne Marketing)

An interesting thing happened when my colleagues at TradeOne Marketing and I first began tracking key copy points in the dealer ads for Sealy Mattress Company. Their dealers had been given a document that identified the key elements of a "perfect" bedding ad. We conducted a sales growth profile analysis of the dealer advertising using the perfect ad elements. Imagine our surprise when we were unable to find any correlation between the use of these elements and high-growth dealers. When we brought the analysis back to the client, the marketing people immediately called the vice president of sales into the room. When exposed to the lack of correlation, the sales vice president explained, "Our best dealers know better than to use those elements called for in a perfect ad. From experience they've learned those elements don't work!" Sealy marketing immediately decided to redefine the elements of a good ad. We used the sales growth profile to establish the optimum advertised price points for mattresses (see Figure 4.4). The analysis revealed which ad elements were in fact driving sales, and that advertising the $99 price point for a twin-bed mattress and $499 for a Posturepedic produced high growth. New ad elements and the power of a $99/$499 price-point strategy was then passed on to dealers.

Showcasing one account's success can light the competitive fires and motivate other accounts to imitate the success (i.e., buy into the manufacturer's program). This type of picture is truly worth a thousand words.

IBM

In the world of desktop computer hardware, price is king. It plays a critical role in generating a retail sale and drives market share. So a marketer must carefully pick the price point to promote a product. The problem is that in the highly competitive marketplace for computers, monitors, and printers, prices are in constant flux.

IBM executives realized the importance of finding the right price points and finding them quickly. Each week, they would see the "street price," or discounted price of merchandise, "footballed" back and forth between competing retailers and manufacturers. IBM marketers needed a mechanism to pinpoint the right prices for products on a weekly basis. Advertising tracking was that mechanism. Competitive ads were clipped, and a system was put into place that tracked the advertised price points of key hardware products. A sample of the kind of reporting this effort produced is illustrated in Figure 4.5.

By tracking competitive advertising to determine that weekend's price points, IBM marketers were able to combat the common practice of bait-and-switch advertising. Many retailers advertised IBM products; however, when customers entered the store looking for an IBM, salespeople switched them to a less expensive—and more cheaply made—product. This product generated a larger profit for the retailer.

Customers might pay a little more for the IBM brand, but they would not pay a substantial amount more. By tracking the advertised competitive price points, IBM marketers were able to adjust their prices in time to compete on a price basis. By adjusting their price points on a weekly basis, IBM strategists were able to rebuild their

FIGURE 4.5 Advertised Retail Price Points

ARE WE PRICE COMPETITIVE?

Brand	Model Name	Chip Type	System Speed	Hard Drive Size	Price/ Share 6/1/97–6/7/97	Sticker shock 6/1/97–6/7/97
DESKTOP: 166 MHz, 2.0–2.5 GB						
Acer	Aspire 2016	Pentium	166 MHz	2 GB	$1,349.99	–$450.00
					5.04%	
Acer	Aspire 2016	Pentium	166 MHz	2 GB	$1,299.99	–$500.00
					5.04%	
Packard Bell	Platinum 2010	Pentium w/MMX	166 MHz	2 GB	$1,399.99	–$400.00
					6.98%	
Packard Bell	Platinum 2010X	Pentium w/MMX	166 MHz	2 GB		
Toshiba	7161	Pentium w/MMX	166 MHz	2.38 GB		
Compaq	Presario 4764	Pentium w/MMX	166 MHz	2.5 GB		
Hewlett Packard	Pavilion 7420	Pentium w/MMX	166 MHz	2.5 GB	$1,699.99	–$100.00
					6.98%	
IBM	Unspecified	Pentium w/MMX	166 MHz	2.5 GB	$1,799.99	
					11.24%	

(Source: ACS TradeOne Marketing)

brand share within the highly competitive desktop computer marketplace. IBM might have reduced prices to be competitive, but the company didn't reduce prices too much. IBM's strategy was to meet or slightly exceed the promotional price points. Any deeper discount would have sacrificed profit margin unnecessarily while also undermining the value of the brand. This precise method of pinpointing prices gave IBM an important strategic advantage over its competitors.

Sometimes having the facts can help a manufacturer maintain the status quo when a channel partner begins to make conclusions that could adversely affect the manufacturer's competitive position. Management at Armstrong responded to a large dealer's questions and kept their promotional dollars working without interruption. Without the information to convince the dealer that promotional dollars were driving sales, a costly interruption in promotional spending could have occurred.

Armstrong Flooring

A major dealer asked Armstrong Flooring for proof that promotional spending led to increased sales. Armstrong marketers felt this request was significant for two reasons. First, Armstrong dealers pay for a portion of the promotional costs. Second, dealers order flooring products to meet consumer demands on a just-in-time basis. Without promotions, Armstrong stood to lose substantial market share.

In the case study, Armstrong had sales and promotional activity at a major dealer tracked for two consecutive quarters. Figure 4.6 shows the results of that tracking. Sales for weeks with promotions were compared with baseline figures for weeks without promotions. The increase in sales with promotions—an average of 54 percent over baseline figures—provided a persuasive argument to the dealer. In fact, the Armstrong sales force also used the data to encourage other dealers to step up their promotional efforts.

The residual effect was even more persuasive. As Figure 4.6 shows, sales not only increased during the promotional period, but also stayed above baseline for most of the quarter. The advertising effect of a promotion was found to continue to drive sales long after the promotion concluded.

FIGURE 4.6 Promotional Effectiveness at Armstrong Flooring, 1996

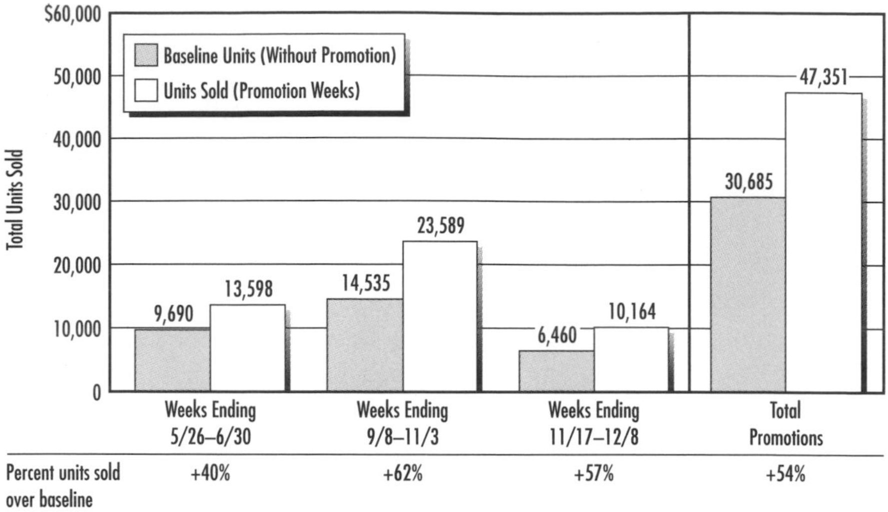

Total Units Sold	Weeks Ending 5/26–6/30	Weeks Ending 9/8–11/3	Weeks Ending 11/17–12/8	Total Promotions
Baseline Units (Without Promotion)	9,690	14,535	6,460	30,685
Units Sold (Promotion Weeks)	13,598	23,589	10,164	47,351
Percent units sold over baseline	+40%	+62%	+57%	+54%

(Source: ACS TradeOne Marketing)

IBM and Armstrong are very focused examples of how information can be used to drive sales in the trade-marketing environment. But not all of the marketing community is eagerly embracing co-marketing as a strategy. Chapter 2 showed how Heinz used branding in the 1970s to increase sales of their ketchup product. In the 1990s, Heinz explored a different approach. It is interesting to note the willingness of this progressive marketing company to be an early adopter once again of an emerging marketing approach and the ire this is generating in the traditional advertising community.

Ad Agencies React to Co-Marketing

As manufacturers and retailers team up in co-marketing efforts, several of these strategic alignments have come under attack.

In 1995, H.J. Heinz announced it was leaving Leo Burnett, its long-time advertising agency, to move to J. Brown/LMC, a trade-oriented agency specializing in co-marketing. Members of the advertising community were aghast. An article in the *New York Times* suggested that Heinz was "siding with those large consumer marketers that are replacing national brand-building image ads with short-term local promotions."

The *Times* story represents the mainline agency view that the tried-and-true, one-size-fits-all media approach is the only way to build brand loyalty. In truth, the established way may be the easiest and least energy-intensive; after all, the ad agency has to produce just one commercial and make only one media buy. But the traditional way is certainly not the *only* way.

"The bottom line is that our marketing focus has changed to reflect a much more targeted approach to reaching our customers," commented a Heinz spokesman. "Broad, full-scale advertising . . . is no longer the best approach for us." Heinz moved instead to account-specific and local market campaigns that blended their corporate message with their retail accounts, even though it took a lot more work than creating one set of ads and running them nationally.

Local promotion campaigns, such as those selected by Heinz, are every bit as "brand-building" as image advertising. In fact, because of the ability to target the audience more precisely, these campaigns can even be more brand-building!

For Your Review

Why consider the Co-Marketing Solution?

- It will integrate the design, administration, and continuous improvement of the trade budget.
- It is set up to consider the individual needs of all channel partners—therefore encouraging their cooperation and trust.
- It incorporates not only co-op advertising, but all trade budgets—a huge sum that should not be left unattended.
- Funneling all spending through a centralized processing source provides the ability to capture data and conduct important analyses.

- The captured data and analyses create a fact-based selling environment. Sales-growth profile analyses provide the facts to convince channel partners which products or promotions will increase their profits.
- Co-marketing helps reestablish credibility with the retailer because the retailer is a major part of the ad's consumer message. Co-marketing not only develops demand for the product, it causes consumers to go to that retailer's store to get the product.

Properly managing the trade-marketing aspect of your business can create win-win situations for you and your channel partners.

5

Valuable Learning from Research

A couple of market research techniques are particularly useful in accurately portraying the trade-market environment: attitude, awareness, and usage (AA&U) research (adapted from consumer-research methods), and field immersion—working with salespeople and personally interviewing key accounts.

An Attitude, Awareness & Usage Study

It is helpful to look at some examples of questions asked in AA&U interviews to see the type of important information that can be gathered and the impact it can have on the strategic planning process.

Tables 5.1 and 5.2 depict a research study in the cellular phone marketplace. The identity of the study's sponsor was concealed to ensure unbiased answers. The AA&U study was conducted among 100 wireless phone buyers.

When I mention* co-op, *which manufacturer's program immediately comes to mind?

The first table shows the manufacturer that was mentioned first (top-of-mind), and the second table records all mentions regardless of order (total awareness). In this example, Cell Phone Co. A dominated the audience in terms of both top-of-mind and total awareness. The finding indicates that the other manufacturers faced a big job.

TABLE 5.1 Co-Op Advertising Program Top-of-Mind (First Mention)

Manufacturer	% All Respondents
Cell Phone Co. A	98
Cell Phone Co. B	1
Cell Phone Co. C	1
Cell Phone Co. D	0
Cell Phone Co. E	0
Cell Phone Co. F	0
Cell Phone Co. G	0
Cell Phone Co. H	0

TABLE 5.2 Co-Op Program Mentions

Manufacturer	% All Respondents
Cell Phone Co. A	100
Cell Phone Co. B	11
Cell Phone Co. C	11
Cell Phone Co. D	11
Cell Phone Co. E	23
Cell Phone Co. F	28
Cell Phone Co. G	2
Cell Phone Co. H	1

On a scale of 1 to 10, with 1 meaning poor and 10 meaning excellent, please rate your overall feelings about each of the programs you mentioned.

Analysis of the responses, as shown in Table 5.3, revealed that Cell Phone Co. A stood head and shoulders above competitors as far

TABLE 5.3 Co-Op Program Ratings (1–10)

Manufacturer	All Respondents
Cell Phone Co. A	7.65
Cell Phone Co. B	5.40
Cell Phone Co. C	7.50
Cell Phone Co. D	7.20
Cell Phone Co. E	5.65
Cell Phone Co. F	6.44
Cell Phone Co. G	5.50
Cell Phone Co. H	7.00

as awareness and positive retailer attitudes. The next questions investigated the reasons why participants liked or disliked programs.

Please tell me what you especially like about programs you rated highly.

The responses to this type of question can express what channel partners are looking for in a co-op program. In this case (see Figure 5.1), it revealed five factors participants liked:

FIGURE 5.1 Likes of Highly Rated Co-Op Programs

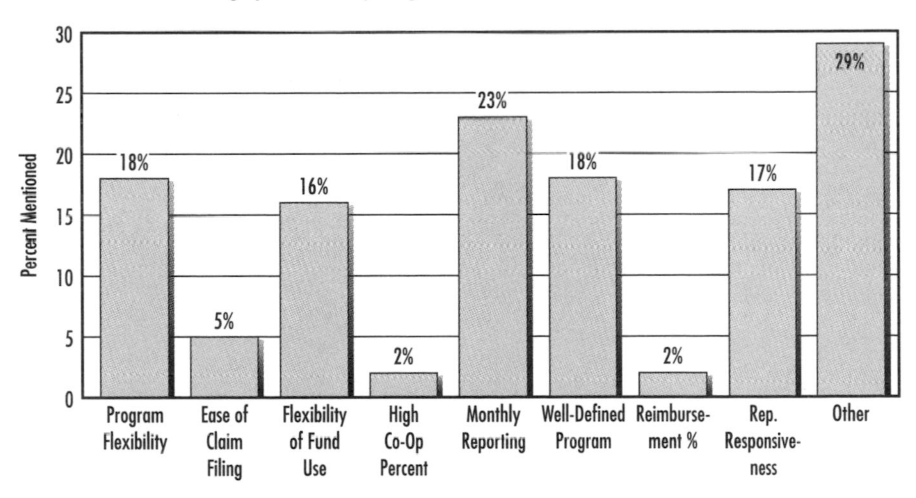

(*Source: ACS TradeOne Marketing*)

1. monthly reports and good communications, 23 percent
2. well-defined program, clearly understood, 18 percent
3. flexible program, 18 percent
4. responsive company representative, 17 percent
5. flexible usage of funds, 16 percent

Conversely, the next question reveals what elements should be avoided in the design of a co-op program meant to motivate channel partners.

Please tell me what you disliked about the programs you rated poorly.

In order of mention, they were

1. no monthly statement, no information about funds, 13 percent
2. too much red tape or paperwork, 12 percent
3. too slow pay, 7 percent
4. too rigid or inflexible, 7 percent

Figure 5.2 shows what participants disliked about the co-op programs they rated poorly.

Significantly, service and communication were deemed more important by program participants than was the level of reimburse-

FIGURE 5.2 Dislikes of Low-Rated Co-Op Programs

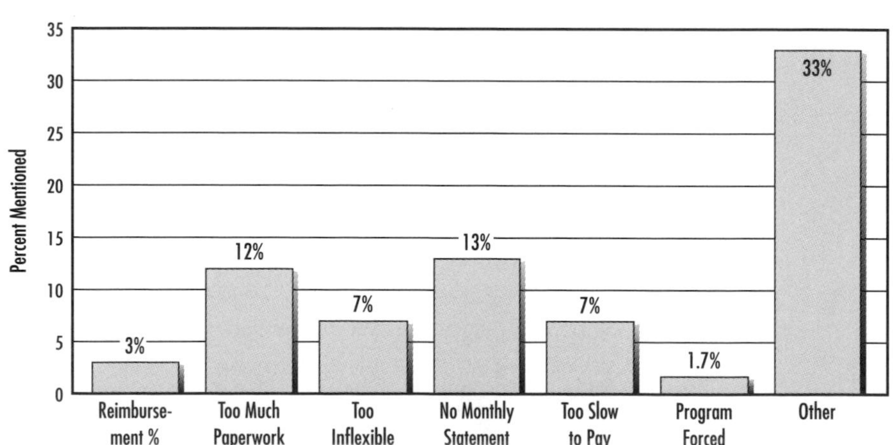

(*Source: ACS TradeOne Marketing*)

ment. This reflects the high degree of leverage that a well-designed, clearly communicated program can have.

Finally, each program is rated in terms of payment levels. This helps answer the question: "Is the program paying more than is needed?"

Would you say the co-op program is:

a. more generous than other programs
b. less generous than other programs
c. about as generous as the average program

In Figure 5.3, the terms of Cell Phone Co. A's program were more generous than the average co-op program. Information such as this might prompt a manufacturer to tighten program guidelines and to require more in terms of performance from participants.

This tightening does not necessarily suggest reducing overall funding or reimbursement levels. Instead, specific branding copy points, price mentions, or benefit mentions might be required for channel partners to qualify for the highest level of reimbursement. Claims that do not include these details would be reimbursed at a lower level, consistent with the competition's payment levels.

AA&U research also can be used to test "trial balloons." Participants can be asked how they would respond to a possible

FIGURE 5.3 Cell Phone Co. A's Cellular Program Relative to Competitors

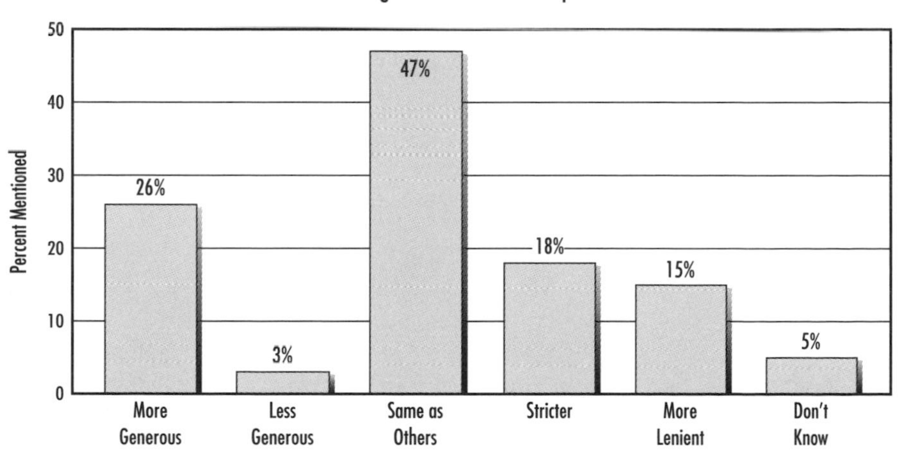

change in the co-op program. Such research can keep a manufacturer from making a big mistake.

In the following example, suppose that company strategists were considering a reduction in their program's claiming period, from any time during the calendar year to 60 days from the time the money was spent. Executives saw this change as a way to encourage participants to claim their available funds faster.

For the co-op program, which of the following statements best expresses your feelings if the claim time were changed to a 60-day period in which to file a claim after the event was run?

a. would like it more
b. would like it less
c. would like it the same
d. would consider dropping
e. don't know

As Figure 5.4 indicates, the proposed program change would have been very unpopular among participants. Information such as this can help the manufacturer avoid painful change, or can provide warning about the expected reaction so that the manufacturer can be prepared to counter the criticism a negative change will generate.

FIGURE 5.4 Opinion Regarding Program Change (60-Day Claim)

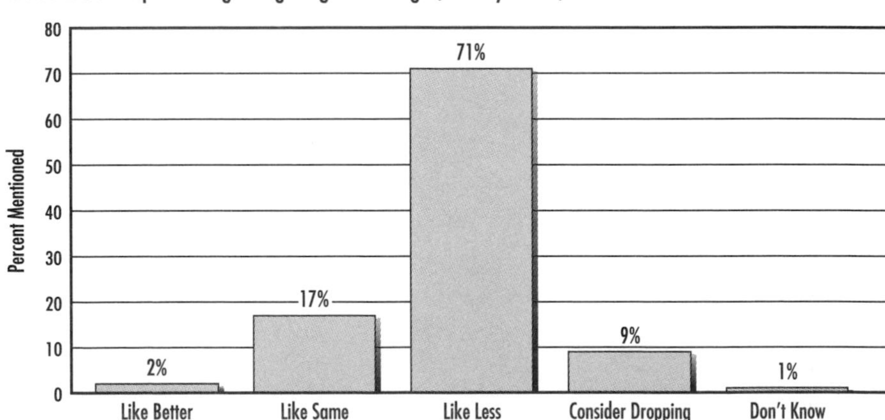

There are numerous other marketing questions the AA&U research can answer. These include, but are not limited to:

- ▲ What kinds of marketing support do big accounts want compared to average-size accounts?
- ▲ What do customers think about the professionalism and friendliness of the salespeople calling on their account?
- ▲ Why are program funds being used the way they are?
- ▲ What problems are customers having in understanding the program and getting paid?
- ▲ How does the program rank versus the competition?
- ▲ Who are the key decision makers regarding how the co-op funds are spent?

One of these questions—"Why are program funds being used the way they are?"—provided crucial information for executives at 3M's Electrical Products Division.

Respondents revealed that the trinkets-and-trash purchases were the easiest way to claim funds before they expired. All it took to claim funds remaining at the end of a program period was to fill out a form. Conversely, respondents indicated that advertising and other market promotions required time for planning and execution—time and expertise that the industrial dealer base didn't always have.

The research generated two possible solutions:

1. Alter the guidelines to give participants more time to use the funds before they expired.
2. Find a way to help participants conduct legitimate marketing events more easily.

Executives rejected the first solution because they wanted their retail partners to invest available funds to stimulate sales. They decided to make it easier for participants to conduct market promotions.

Their Promotion-in-a-Box program did just that. Comprised of prepackaged promotional material, the program included a series of in-store offers with displays that featured giveaway items, like work gloves and ice chests, along with samples of 3M products. The dealer could order these giveaway items, the product display to promote them, and collateral materials simply by checking a box on a form.

3M Uses Market Research to Find a New Way

The Electrical Products Division of 3M was interested in turbo-charging their co-op program. The existing program that had been in place for a number of years was not motivating accounts in the way 3M management desired. A number of dealers, for example, used co-op funds to buy 3M merchandise (e.g., hats and shirts) rather than to promote 3M products. Management wanted to know why many of their dealers were using the co-op funds to buy promotional items such as hats and T-shirts, commonly referred to as trinkets and trash. They were concerned because their co-op program was not generating sufficient awareness and demand for 3M products. The AA&U gave them the answers.

3M executives wanted to know why their co-op program wasn't working as intended and what was needed to support their products more effectively in the marketplace. To this end, an AA&U survey was conducted among a random sample of about 100 participants in the 3M co-op program.

Contacted via telephone, respondents were asked standardized questions about their attitudes toward co-op programs in general. They were not informed which of the manufacturers had commissioned the study. Analysis of the survey revealed that the 3M program rated comparatively highly. Regarding the use of funds to buy trinkets and trash, retailers indicated this expenditure was a very easy way to quickly spend available funds that were about to expire.

The respondents expressed an interest in using the co-op money to execute more effective marketing promotions. But they also indicated they lacked the time and expertise to put together these promotions. This concern was especially prevalent among the small and midsize accounts. Unlike large accounts, these accounts lacked the resources required to implement sophisticated marketing projects (e.g., direct mail, telemarketing, or displays containing strong consumer offers).

After careful study, a program called Promotion-in-a-Box was recommended. It contained mass-customizable, prepackaged promotions that could be tailored to meet the needs of an individual retailer or wholesale distributor. The program made a number of different display promotions as easy to order as trinkets and trash. The turnkey promotions required very little work from the retailer. Accounts would just have to check boxes and fill in blanks to order and supply information about the target market, the store, and the desired promotional offer.

Figure 5.5 shows how easy it was to order direct-mail, telemarketing, and display programs. A promotional display offered to electrical component purchasers is shown in Figure 5.6. 3M's prepackaged display promotions produced excellent results.

During the next year, over 60 percent of the participants' co-op funds shifted to Promotion-in-a-Box orders. The increase in marketing effectiveness was so directly related to higher sales that 3M increased the budget for their co-op advertising program the following year by a staggering 100 percent.

The 3M Promotion-in-a-Box program was subsequently submitted as an entry in an industry contest. Judges awarded it a prize for market effectiveness and creativity.

FIGURE 5.5 Promotion-in-a-Box

Program Enhancement

Telemarketing	Direct Mail	Point-of-Sale Kits
# of calls 200	# of mailers 2,500	Which promotion ____
Business Type ______	Business Type ______	Promo dates ______
SIC Code ______	SIC Code ______	▲ donut ads ______
Geographic area ____	Geographic area ____	▲ banners ______
Business size ______	Business size ______	▲ counter props ____
Target dates ______	Target drop date ____	Additional materials
Info captured ______	Ad slicks needed ____	______
Add your customers	Add your customers	______
______	______	______
______	______	______
▲ Lead qualifying	▲ Sales prospecting	▲ Premium placement
▲ Closing sales	▲ New product intro	▲ Special promotions
▲ Direct mail follow-up	▲ Special promotions	▲ Specific product push

(Source: ACS TradeOne Marketing)

FIGURE 5.6 3M Promotion-in-a-Box

(Source: ACS TradeOne Marketing)

For the dealer, the Promotion-in-a-Box program made promotion planning and fulfillment as easy as ordering T-shirts. The program gave the dealer every item necessary to run each promotion, including prepackaged displays.

A year after the program was introduced, nearly 60 percent of the co-op budget was skewed to Promotion-in-a-Box spending. The plan had successfully redirected co-op funds toward more effective demand-pull promotional activity. The Promotion-in-a-Box program was so successful in driving sales growth that executives doubled its overall spending level the following year!

Survey results do not always produce such dramatic results. Sometimes field research—interviews with customers and salespeople—generates remarkable answers to questions about the quantitative data.

Field Immersion Reveals a Win for Harley-Davidson

Spending time in the field working with some of Harley-Davidson's best salespeople proved quite revealing. The time I spent visiting top dealers and discussing what types of marketing events were driving business provided the key to unlocking a major opportunity for the durable-goods manufacturer. Everyone knows what a strong brand name Harley has. The Harley dealers like to say that their brand name is so strong that customers actually tattoo it on their bodies. High praise indeed! But what other manufacturers and charities were willing to do to get Harley's product involved in their promotional activities was nothing short of amazing.

In repeated visits with Harley sales managers and dealers, a common theme began to emerge. Stories of the offers that were made to dealers if they would contribute a motorcycle to a promotion were astounding:

- In Houston, Coca-Cola would spend over $250,000 in media support and hold a drawing for all ticket holders from a series of Houston Astros baseball games. If area dealers would contribute a motorcycle, they could participate in the promotion and ticket holders could be directed to their stores.

- In Dallas, the Muscular Dystrophy Association sponsors an annual duck race at White Rock Lake. Ducks were "purchased" with a contestant number at local retailers for $5. Eight weeks of media support ensured that virtually every man, woman, and child within 50 miles would know about this event. Harley dealers were asked to contribute a motorcycle as first prize. Consumers were directed to dealer stores to purchase ducks. A local builder offered a new home as first prize. The sponsors chose the Harley motorcycle instead!

When questioned, Harley salespeople and dealers in other cities had similar stories to share. Stories of the major promotional opportunities that they were asked to participate in were prevalent. Most of them passed up the offers, however, since the Harley-Davidson product was on allocation and dealers were preselling any bikes they could get their hands on. On occasion, headquarters would advance an extra motorcycle to help the dealers out, but this was more the exception than the rule. The result was that Harley-Davidson was missing out on many opportunities to capitalize on the amazing aura surrounding their brand name.

Harley-Davidson's top marketing people quickly grasped the potential this phenomenon represented. Contributing a motorcycle with a $25,000 manufacturer's suggested retail price could yield $250,000 to $400,000 worth of measured media exposure. And the opportunities to partner with leading charities further reinforced the brand's position as a responsible member of the community. Senior marketers saw the wisdom of redirecting some of their consumer advertising funds, if necessary, to take advantage of this unusual opportunity.

Harley-Davidson developed an innovative co-marketing program to give Harley dealers and salespeople a budget to fund these types of opportunities. A formal system to apply for these funds and involve the corporate marketing department in the program design was developed and implemented.

The opportunity to get a 10-to-1 return on the marketing dollars would never have been recognized if it weren't for the time spent riding with salespeople and visiting with key dealers. This part of the process also created excellent buy-in for the new program. Since the new program came directly out of the desires of the field, it also reinforced the fact that Harley-Davidson management was listening to the field and respected what they had to contribute. This type of respect and relationship building is an important by-product gained from face-to-face field interviews in the selling environment.

For Your Review

What to consider in attitude, awareness, and usage (AA&U) research:

- Keep the identity of your company concealed until the questions have been answered.
- Find out what partners expect from a co-op program: what do they like and dislike about the co-op programs they participate in.
- Have them rate the co-op programs they know.
- Find out their opinions about your co-op program.
- Use the study to "field test" possible changes you would like to incorporate into your co-op program.
- Find out why your partners use their co-op funds the way they do.

What you can gain from working in the field with salespeople and interviewing key accounts:

- personal accounts of the impact of your brand's name
- opportunities to further strengthen or profit from your brand's image
- reinforcement of respect and relationship building with your partners
- buy-in from the sales force for the new programs because their opinions are incorporated

Research in your trade-market environment is extremely valuable to your company.

6

The Power of Fact-Based Selling

The Co-Marketing Solution pools a large amount of data gathered from various sources. Individually, the data does very little to direct the co-marketing strategy. But pieced together, these data can present a clear picture from which to derive that strategy.

At the heart of the Co-Marketing Solution lies a sophisticated computer system that tracks all claims and spending associated with the co-marketing plan. In addition to paying claims, the system captures valuable marketing data. Database technology and careful programming result in a system that can track and correlate useful spending information for each account, such as the following:

- media spending patterns
- sales patterns
- price points
- ad content, copy points, and marketing messages
- promotional offers
- in-store activity
- brand messaging and logo usage

By consolidating this information through a central source, account-specific data becomes available in one place. Analysis of these data can yield valuable marketing intelligence such as the following:

- ▲ total spending as a percent of sales for each account
- ▲ the relative value of different types of promotions
- ▲ how the fast-growth accounts are spending funds
- ▲ the advertising messages used by fast-growth accounts
- ▲ price points that drive consumer interest
- ▲ product offers that provide higher profit margins

Once derived, this marketing intelligence can be used to promote the desired behavior among program participants. That is, program guidelines can be updated to reward those activities that generate desired results. In the world of trade marketing, knowing what the company wants to have happen gives the executives the control to make it happen.

Such intelligence can be a valuable tool for salespeople. Armed with account-specific information, a salesperson can review an account's marketing expenditures and the results these expenditures achieve. To make a compelling case, a salesperson can compare one account's sales growth and spending patterns with others. An account that grew only 12 percent, for example, should be very interested in the ways other accounts spent their money to achieve 40 percent growth.

By bringing valuable information to the retailer, the salesperson creates a basis for a new type of relationship. In essence, this is a return to the "good old days" when the retailer depended upon the manufacturer for information. Only now, the data provided by the manufacturer has become far more sophisticated.

The salesperson can take the role of promotional planner for the account, developing promotional and merchandising strategies. Working closely together with key accounts on such plans produces two major advantages for the manufacturer.

The first is obvious. Becoming involved in promotional planning shifts the salesperson's focus from sell-in to sell-through. That focus on the retailer's goals usually results in increases in the retail movement of the manufacturer's product.

The second advantage is less obvious, but nonetheless very important. The new focus on sell-through begins the process of building the credibility that salespeople lost over the years. A bond is once again created with key accounts. This bond can lead to valuable intangibles, such as the opportunity to assist the buyer in planning the entire category. Other intangibles include "first looks" at the retailer's promotional goals and the opportunity to be the featured brand in key promotions.

By bringing valuable data to the table, the salesperson becomes a strategic consultant who can help to maximize sales of an entire category. The credibility and respect gained through this approach cannot be overstated. Creating a fact-based selling environment moves channel activity from glad-handing sales to focused market planning.

In the 1950s and 1960s, manufacturers built strong relationships with the trade by providing data on product movement. In the upcoming decade, manufacturers have the opportunity once again to build strong bonds by offering trade-spending information. Forward-thinking manufacturers will seize this opportunity and leapfrog those who don't.

In the long run, it is likely that all manufacturers will learn the wisdom of investing in the strategic management of the trade budget from a market-driven viewpoint. The companies who learn this lesson sooner rather than later will lead the pack. The innovators will derive a relationship power that will entrench their products in the retailers' strategic plans. For early adopters, this strategic opportunity will be as major in scope as the 1960s' branding revolution was in the consumer packaged-goods category. And the power of the co-marketing approach is not limited to consumer packaged goods; it's applicable to every product category that relies on an intermediary between manufacturer and end-user.

Influencing Trade Partners

Influence in the form of valuable sell-through information knows no chain of command when it comes to trade marketing. It works by bringing important marketing information and planning assistance to the retail partner. Meaningful information (e.g., fact-based data conveying best-practice strategies) can leverage the trade partner's ability to sell more of the manufacturer's product and create a win-win situation.

Marketers influence their trade partners primarily through positive reinforcement. Punitive measures almost always backfire in the world of trade marketing. Key elements of the consumer strategy should be presented in the program guidelines and proper branding messages should be recognized and rewarded.

It should be very clear to the trade partner that reimbursement levels are higher for messages that include preferred branding, pricing, and positioning and why.

- If trade partners run the co-op program according to the manufacturer's guidelines, their expenditures should be reimbursed at higher levels.
- If trade partners insist on doing things their own way—and many will—expenditures should be reimbursed at lower levels.
- If the messages (stated or implied) erode corporate strategy, their expenditures should not be reimbursed at any level.

It is important to support the different reimbursement levels with data that correlates the value of marketing messages to sales results. Savvy trade partners will understand why a manufacturer would invest more in advertising or promotions that have been proven effective. A manufacturer may offer to reimburse 75 percent—or even 100 percent—of trade partners' costs for these proved messages, compared to the standard 50 percent.

Besides tinkering with guidelines and reimbursement levels, marketers must find as many ways to partner with retailers and distributors as proved feasible. (Retailers do not take kindly to manufacturers who attempt to impose programs on them with too heavy a hand.) In fact, each relationship that develops while planning promotions and sharing corporate strategies will evolve over time and be far more important than what can be accomplished on just one sales call.

The Importance of Communication

American businesses invest a lot in communication. Big dollars are spent on advertising agencies who expertly communicate corporate strategies to targeted consumers. In addition to reaching the target market with a message, clients expect consumers to enjoy and like the message.

Similarly, corporations spend big dollars on public relations (PR) firms who have elevated communication to an art form. Messages that PR firms spin can defuse potentially damaging situations. Both PR and corporate executives recognize the importance of thoughtful communication for restoring confidence when the company faces a negative circumstance.

Those manufacturing executives who understand the power of co-marketing insist on first-class communications with their trade partners. These executives consider each trade account an untapped market opportunity. As a result, they view each trade partner as a prospect for marketing strategy; so they call in the experts—trade-oriented promotion agencies and the PR firms—to help them communicate effectively with trade partners.

Trade partners appreciate the professional copy-writing and audiovisual programming on more than one level. First, they are grateful for clear, thoughtful guidelines that reduce disagreements and demonstrate an awareness of their concerns. Second, they understand that the effort and attention to detail demonstrates that the manufacturer recognizes their importance. Third, crisp reports and competitive analyses on specific promotional activities reinforce the stated intent: by sharing knowledge and know-how, both the manufacturer and the trade partners profit.

These ongoing working relationships will pay off in the long run. Even if a trade partner occasionally fails to adopt a manufacturer's strategy, a mutual appreciation of one another will keep hope alive for future campaigns.

The real breakthrough occurs when strategies coincide. The time spent sharing pertinent information provides an opportunity for the manufacturer and the retailer to co-promote one another effectively. This process of working together as equal partners toward a common strategic goal encapsulates the true benefit of the co-marketing strategy. This strategy creates partners where adversaries once existed.

Information is the key to jump-starting relationships with trade partners. Retailers and distributors love to compete against one another. They thrive on it. Tapping into this primary motivation (e.g., by relating the success of a category or a brand at a major competitor) will often spur retailers into action. Data and analyses of successful marketing strategies and insights into competitors' situations make the salesperson extremely influential.

By assisting in a retailer's small victory over the competition, the salesperson helps the trade partner sell more units and solidifies the partnership between manufacturer and retailer. Win-win scenarios are good for business. Fact-based selling provides a new and very different environment in which to compete.

The New Role of the Salesperson

In the product-oriented environment of the 1950s to mid-1980s, the salesperson was like a visiting emissary. He or she visited customers (channel partners) bearing samples, demonstrating new products, and writing orders. The salesperson then returned to the office, filled out expense accounts, checked the status of orders, and learned about the new products his or her employer was offering.

In the service economy of the 1990s, the salesperson is no longer a wandering emissary. Instead, the salesperson must function within the organization to help coordinate and manage cross-departmental project teams that work to fulfill a customer's order. More complex than in times past, today's order usually resembles more a solution to a problem than a straightforward list of goods to be delivered. In addition to the product, today's order often includes services (e.g., to install the product or to train personnel in using the product). This is especially true in higher-margin, more profitable situations.

The salesperson has transformed from an emissary presenting his wares to a quarterback calling the plays. Working with representatives within different departments of the channel partner's organization, the salesperson returns to help his or her in-house customer team to fully understand the relationship of their product to the customer's need. The salesperson coordinates the activities of all team members in order to deliver the total solution. In the new selling environment of service and solutions, the salesperson orchestrates the delivery of customer satisfaction. The higher the customer sat, the more loyal the relationship. Solving a customer's problem and creating customer satisfaction are closely intertwined in the new service-based economy.

The Co-Marketing Solution arms the salesperson with new, valuable information. This knowledge levels the playing field in the manufacturer and retailer's relationship. No longer the annoying vendor, the salesperson emerges as the prized consultant, one whose information can accelerate sell-through and category growth.

This new leverage is needed to offset another fact in today's fast-paced manufacturing world. With knockoff products being introduced at alarming speeds, it has become very difficult for salespeople to establish product differences. It has become equally difficult to make mainstream consumers aware of these differences. By the time product difference is established, competitors have copied the product, mitigating the advantage.

As a result of this fact of life, the salesperson's information and knowledge may be all that differentiates the manufacturer's product from the competition. The salesperson who helps the retailer sell more product and helps the retailer make decisions to optimize the entire category, sets his or her company apart. Figure 6.1 shows information that can be provided to a channel partner. Imagine the effect such information has on the customer.

Today, buyers are equipped with high-tech information management systems that can instantly provide them with sales information. But they don't know what share of promotional and advertising space a specific product is receiving. They don't know how target consumers react to different promotional dynamics such as price points, product features, and promotional offers.

As retailers move from ad to ad, they fail to track the overall impact of what they are promoting and the relative effect it has on driving sell-through. By providing retailers with the information they lack, the salesperson becomes a strategic partner of the retailer. Such salespeople participate in the retailer's planning process, rather than just the buying process. Reports that break down sales of the manufacturers' products are invaluable for helping the salesperson justify a specific product's need for more shelf space and advertising support.

Figure 6.1 is taken from the jeans category.

FIGURE 6.1a Retailer A—Jeans*

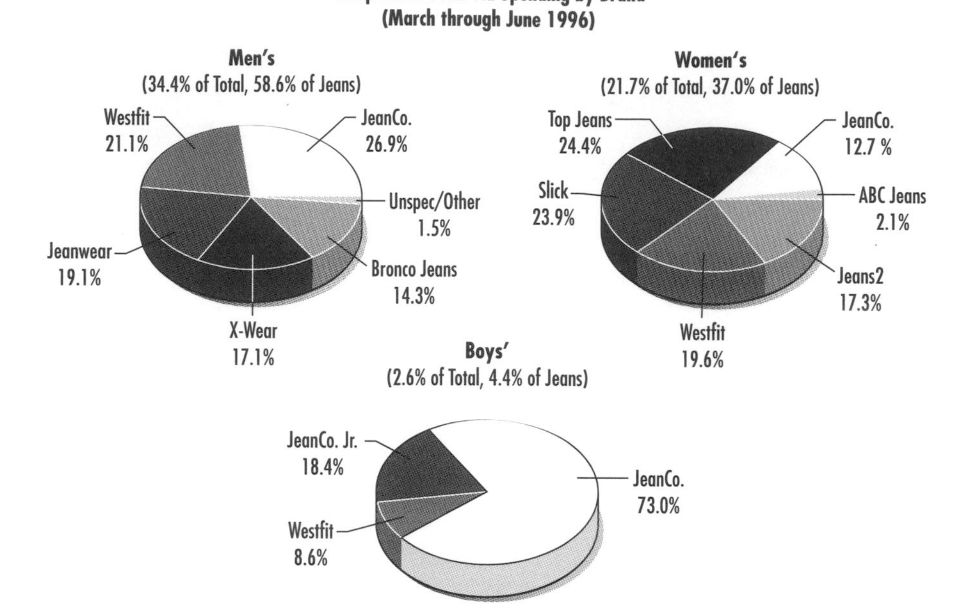

FIGURE 6.1b Do Account Promotions Drive Sales?*

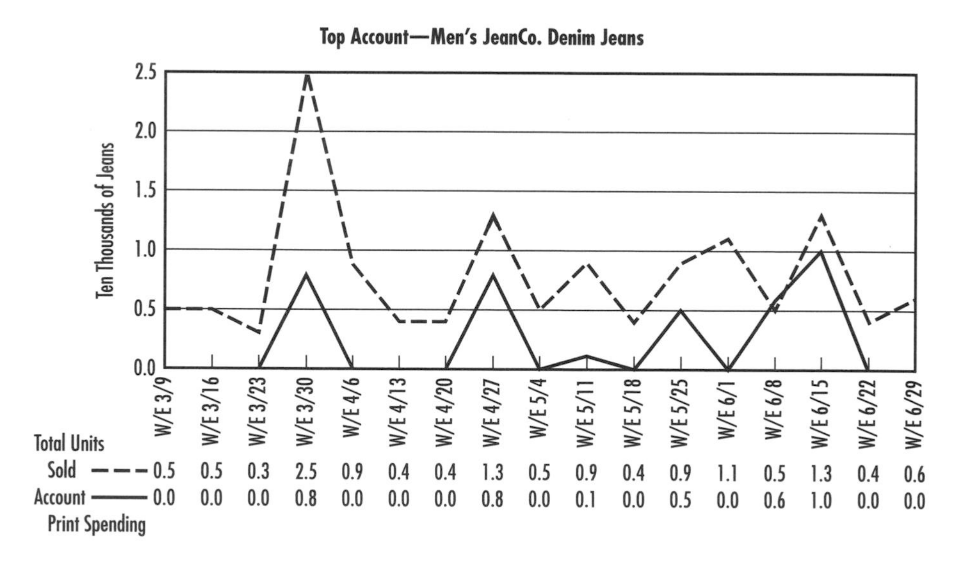

	W/E 3/9	W/E 3/16	W/E 3/23	W/E 3/30	W/E 4/6	W/E 4/13	W/E 4/20	W/E 4/27	W/E 5/4	W/E 5/11	W/E 5/18	W/E 5/25	W/E 6/1	W/E 6/8	W/E 6/15	W/E 6/22	W/E 6/29
Total Units Sold - - -	0.5	0.5	0.3	2.5	0.9	0.4	0.4	1.3	0.5	0.9	0.4	0.9	1.1	0.5	1.3	0.4	0.6
Account Print Spending ———	0.0	0.0	0.0	0.8	0.0	0.0	0.0	0.8	0.0	0.1	0.0	0.5	0.0	0.6	1.0	0.0	0.0

FIGURE 6.1c Print Advertising Spending by Segment*

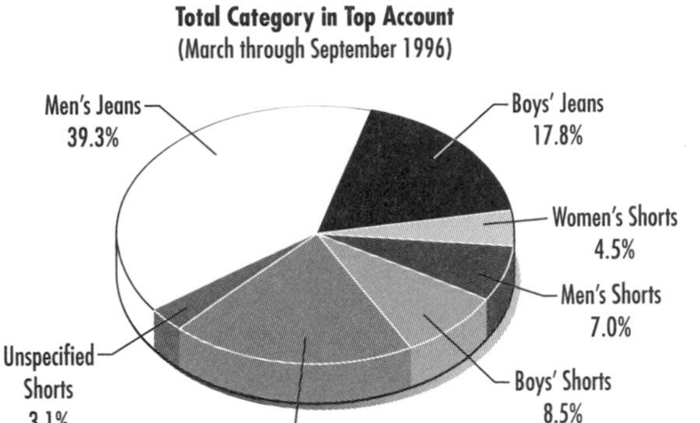

FIGURE 6.1d Jeans*

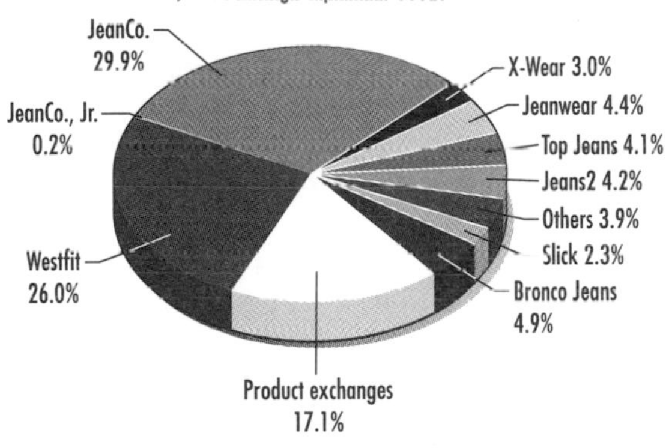

**Fictional data*

Figures 6.1a–d are examples of reports used to break down sales of manufacturers' products.

This summary report allows the salesperson to share with the buyer very valuable information about how the category is being promoted. The report quantifies the amount of promotional support that each manufacturer is receiving and supports the case for more or different activity. By providing information on all competitive products, the salesperson helps the buyer maximize far more than the sales of just one product. By supplying a broad perspective, the salesperson can help the buyer boost sales of the entire category.

Buena Vista Records

Executives at Buena Vista Records were worried about the frequent out-of-stock conditions that existed at some of the largest mass merchants. They traced the problem to their difficulty in securing and holding shelf space commensurate with their market share. They were without effective data to show market demand by product type for both their products and their competitors' products. It looked as if the shelf space problem would continue—along with the problem of out-of-stock conditions and the resulting lost sales—until data was generated to prove their point.

Working with Best Buy, Buena Vista developed that data through a pilot program. The partners decided to examine the effectiveness of different merchandising options by tracking advertising and gathering in-store sales data. The program helped Buena Vista marketers successfully demonstrate to Best Buy buyers the impact that advertising, promoting, and displaying Buena Vista products had on positive overall category management.

An amazing payoff was that Buena Vista marketers were invited by Best Buy to participate in regular planning sessions for category activities, including shelf space allocation.

For Your Review

The old adage "knowledge is power" has never been truer than when applied to trade marketing. By using the Co-Marketing

Solution, forward-looking companies arm their salespeople with crucial information, and elevate them from their prior vendor status:

- Salespeople are able to work closely with accounts as promotional planners, gaining first "looks" at the accounts' promotional goals, and opportunities to be the featured brand in key promotions.
- Salespeople's focus has changed from sell-in to sell-through. With information concerning the impact of promotional dynamics and advertising, salespeople serve as consultants for trade partners, increasing retail movement of the product.
- Salespeople become problem solvers, working with all the retailer's team members to increase sales and category growth.
- Salespeople regain the manufacturer's lost credibility, creating bonds with key accounts.

Are your salespeople prized consultants that set your company apart? Or are they merely visiting emissaries presenting your wares?

Tips for influencing your trade partners:

- Provide them with meaningful information that increases their abilities to sell your products and increase profits all around.
- Use information about competition to help your trade partners increase their profits.
- Communicate with your trade partners on a professional level, assuring them of your partnership, respect, and mutual profit.
- Partner with your retailers and distributors in as many ways as possible. Working together toward a strategic goal is more effective than forcefully imposing programs.
- Inform your trade partners that reimbursement levels will be higher for co-op programs run according to your company's guidelines. Explain that your guidelines are set up according to the advertising or promotions that are most effective.

- Realize that punitive measures will backfire. But from the beginning, make it clear to your partners that your company will not reimburse advertising that damages your corporate strategy.

The Co-Marketing Solution provides a fact-based selling environment, invaluable for strengthening your relationships with your trade partners.

7

Co-Marketing and the Category Killers

Sales Dollars Versus Profit Margins

In today's environment of corporate restructuring and category-killer retailers, such as Wal-Mart and Home Depot, many manufacturers have fallen into what may be called the "key-account trap." This trap occurs when corporate strategists, in an attempt to streamline cost of operations, decide to focus on the 20 percent of distribution that accounts for 80 percent of their sales. Rather than serve 2,000 channel partners, they reason that serving just 400 partners would significantly reduce the demands on their sales, customer support, and billing departments. With fewer customers, strategists might also point out that they could concentrate better on exactly what this smaller set of customers really wants.

Of course, the key-account trap may tempt strategists in a few years to focus on the 10 percent of the customers that account for 90 percent of sales. The trap snaps shut when the manufacturer limits their direct selling relationships to only very large customers. The manufacturer usually doesn't stop doing business with other customers, but these customers are turned over to third-party distributors, reps, or brokers. When moved from direct distribution to two-step distribution, these customers become "second-class citizens" as far as co-op advertising and co-marketing programs are concerned.

The logic for reducing the number of customers appears to be sound. But before succumbing to this line of thinking, it is important to consider some important strategic factors.

- **Relative profit margin:**
  Mass merchants and category killers negotiate hard for the lowest price. Their immense buying power combined with the high demand for their shelf space enables them to negotiate the best deals. In fact, many purchase-order agreements stipulate "best pricing," guaranteeing these large accounts the lowest price.

  Midsize accounts, on the other hand, do not enjoy the same buying power and are accustomed to paying a higher price. While the large accounts may contribute the highest percentage of overall sales and profit dollars, the midsize accounts usually generate a higher overall profit as a percentage of sales.

- **Leverage loss:**
  Large accounts enjoy the luxury of commanding, "My way or take the highway!" Midsize accounts, conversely, welcome partnering and listen to the needs of the manufacturer. Midsize accounts respect the size of the large manufacturer and appreciate any attention they may receive. Large accounts expect and demand both attention and the best price and yet remain very difficult to work with.

- **Full-line distribution:**
  Large accounts make their product decisions based on very strict shelf movement and profit contribution guidelines, and practice just-in-time ordering methods. As a result, maintaining full-line distribution proves very difficult for the manufacturer. Usually, the best-selling items are "cherry picked" from the lines of each manufacturer.

  On the other hand, midsize accounts, in order to coexist with the category killers, focus on delivering a higher level of customer satisfaction, which includes greater selection. In addition to full-line distribution, this emphasis means that midsize accounts carry the manufacturer's higher priced and more profitable products.

- **New-product life:**
Products in large accounts attract the attention of people other than potential consumers. They also attract the attention of copycat manufacturers. These firms quickly knock off the new products and sell them for less.

The visibility at large accounts shortens the already brief life cycle of new products, making it difficult to generate a good return on the investment in research and development. In contrast, midsize accounts provide fertile ground for new product testing. They also make good long-term venues for low-volume, premium-priced products.

Before executives at a company abdicate the second tier to distributors, they should pay close attention to the strategic role these accounts can play in product life cycles, product testing, profit margins, and the breadth of product lines.

When all of a manufacturer's accounts are "600-pound gorillas," it is difficult to feed them all without hungering for profits. My experience has been that the executives of a manufacturing organization who choose to concentrate exclusively on the large retailers often regret it. They become addicted to large accounts and big orders, and this "narcotic" drives their decision-making. Eventually, a large retailer will play hardball with the manufacturer. Then the search for the next new product for Kmart or Target becomes a life-and-death struggle.

When determining appropriate goals for your trade marketing program, it is helpful to consider the profitability of each tier of distribution. Acknowledging the differences in these tiers leads to the development of three different approaches to maximize the opportunity with each account type:

1. **Key-account plan:** This plan should be structured and yet flexible, allowing for the custom development of a plan for each large account. By taking a disciplined approach to planning and understanding each account, manufacturing executives promote

consistency and success in their co-marketing programs. By allowing for differences between accounts, the plan provides for the individual attention that such important business partners deserve.

2. **Second-tier plan:** In keeping with the needs of these highly profitable, strategic accounts, the second-tier plan should feature a heavy dose of marketing assistance. These accounts welcome the opportunity to partner and co-market, especially with co-branding programs. Don't overlook the value and power of strong regional accounts.

3. **Standard co-op:** The plan for the remaining midsize and small accounts should use a cookie-cutter approach, featuring standard, easy-to-administer guidelines. Offering some support to these accounts can build solid relationships and pay off in the future with those that grow to be large.

If distributors participate in the management of these accounts, the manufacturer's plan should provide and insist upon a high quality of service and support to ensure that the potential of these accounts is still realized. The plan also should allow the manufacturer to work closely with distributor-managed accounts on joint-marketing initiatives.

It is very important to clearly define what constitutes a second-tier account and how it differs from other accounts. These definitions will help reduce confusion in the future. The power large accounts have is already daunting. Improperly managed, it can overwhelm almost any manufacturer. As such, it is important for manufacturers to employ strategies to closely manage these relationships and to make sure that their distribution channels remain vibrant enough to support their overall business strategies.

Key-Account Planning Model

The most effective way to work with major accounts is one-on-one. Key-account planning enables a manufacturer to develop a custom marketing plan with each account. The retailer wants only two things: to increase category sales and to reduce costs. Large retailers do not want to participate in promotions available to their competition. They prefer to work with an exclusive offer that they can use to drive store volume and foot traffic of their own stores at the expense of their competitors. Implementing a program that can be customized for each large retailer or channel partner is the solution to working well with large accounts.

Manufacturers should follow one of the two basic models for conducting key-account planning:

1. **Trust model:** Develop a promotional plan and allow the account to deduct the cost of that plan from the order placed. Some accounts will also accept payment in extra product (this is helpful for cash-starved manufacturers).

2. **Transaction model:** Develop a promotional plan, document it, and agree to fund it upon proof-of-performance received from the account. The proof is a claim with documentation for the promotional services agreed upon and the cost paid for these services.

As its name implies, the first model assumes the manufacturer can trust the retailer to use the discount to implement agreed-upon promotional activities. Sometimes this trust is rewarded. Other times, the retailer just takes the discount as an additional profit without conducting the incremental demand pull promotional activity. If the manufacturer fails to monitor the activity closely, retailers will eventually move back to their preferred method of operating, i.e., take the discount to profit or price reduction.

The transaction model documents the agreement, proof-of-performance, and payment. This model also provides the paper trail to track results. When the claim is submitted, the retailer also can be required to submit sales results to validate the effectiveness of the promotional activity. Typically, the largest accounts refuse to provide proof-of-performance documentation. If a manufacturer wants to gain access to the information needed to understand and evaluate what the retailer is actually doing with their money, it is necessary to take extra steps.

Some manufacturers with the insight and resources have taken the approach of making it as easy as they can for retailers to work with them, while providing the ability to measure the amount of actual support they are receiving. Companies like Intel Corporation implement advertising tracking systems that measure the support each large retailer gives them and then makes automatic payments based on this activity. They also invest in services that will track inventory and sell-through levels at the retailer, so they can correlate advertising and promotion support with product sell-through. Investing in these types of tracking and measurement systems is the most effective way of working with the largest retailers. Large manufacturers like Procter & Gamble understand the value of such systems and make the investment to gather the data they need to manage these relationships with key accounts on a factual basis.

A manufacturer with limited marketing funds cannot afford to not know whether promotions are successful in moving product. If a promotion proves unsuccessful, excess product sold at a discount will sit in inventory and detract from future sales. Therefore, a transaction-based program tying marketing activity to each order is the preferred method. If a manufacturer is fortunate to work with a buyer who will cooperate, a salesperson can plan and fund demand-generating events individually designed to move a particular large order off the retailer's shelf.

Creating and Satisfying Retailer Demand-Pull Activity

To be successful, salespeople from smaller companies must learn how to tap into some of the not-so-subtle factors that motivate buyers of their products at large retailers.

Many large retailers set up and track promotional areas—including displays, catalogs, trade shows, and circulars—as profit centers. Buyers and merchandising people are offered incentives to sell manufacturers on these extra "services." Salespeople shouldn't be surprised if buyers and merchandising managers push these services hard. Salespeople must be prepared to buy some of these services if they expect retailers to buy their products. It's a cost of doing business.

It is up to the salespeople to manage these situations proactively. They must evaluate the potential of each marketing option. The scarce marketing dollars of a small company cannot be wasted—they must drive sales.

The following methods are worthy of consideration for driving sales:

- ▲ partially fund a temporary price decrease to hit an important consumer price point
- ▲ pay the redemption on a mail-in, consumer rebate coupon that is delivered at the store level
- ▲ obtain display space sufficient in size to guarantee that additional product is ordered
- ▲ place the retailer's logo in the manufacturer's product advertising to let consumers know where to buy the product
- ▲ offer a sales incentive paid directly to the person who sold the product

When making the frequent decisions of what to fund and what to pass on, it is helpful for salespeople to have accurate information regarding what works and what doesn't in driving sales.

The Small-Business Dilemma

Co-marketing principles can work for small businesses just as they do for corporations with large branding budgets. But marketers must be prepared to modify old paradigms.

At one time, building awareness through consumer advertising was the only model considered when a company launched a new product or promoted the sale of an existing product. But my experience with a midsize computer software company made me question this conventional wisdom. I found that while the old model was successful in building demand, retailers refused to stock sufficient quantities to meet the demand. Thus out-of-stock conditions were created at some major retail accounts.

The DacEasy Story

DacEasy created the low-price, computer software category. An enterprising marketer named Kevin Howe saw the opportunity in the mid-1980s to sell accounting software to small businesses in a brand-new way. Studying the economics of computer software, Kevin noted that once the development work had been completed, the cost of the software product itself was very small. In fact, it was usually just the cost of copying a disk, providing a manual, and advertising and shipping the product. Kevin decided to try a whole new method of distribution. He worked with developers to integrate the accounting function so it could fit on one or two floppy disks. To create awareness and distribution, Kevin decided to use mass-marketing techniques. He ran magazine ads offering the product direct for only $69. The response was amazing. Product that normally would cost over $1,000 and be delivered by an accounting professional was now available at throwaway pricing. The first month, DacEasy sold more units of accounting software than had been sold during the entire previous year. This created a whole new category of financial software products.

After a few years, the popularity of DacEasy had grown to the point where retailers asked to carry the product. Eventually the original product plus networked versions were available through direct mail, retail, and consultants known as value added resellers. Distribution had matured, and many competitors were in the shelf space, as well. Marketing and promotion had become essential to holding shelf space in an increasingly competitive retail environment. I was asked to see what I could do to help, and my immediate response was to rely on the demand-generating model I had come to know and love.

After repackaging the line to give it a contemporary look and a product line look, it was time to generate new orders and sell-through. I put together a marketing plan composed of national advertising, retail promotion, and coupons. Of course, this was implemented through our marketing department, and we expected retailers to fall in line and stock the product for us. We received opening orders, and everything seemed to go well as our sell-in product reached the shelves. Imagine my surprise three weeks later when I visited large computer stores and found that the product we had shipped had completely moved through, but it had not been replaced with reorders of DacEasy. Instead, the buyer had replaced our product with that of a competitor who offered another promotional price. The demand we were still generating for accounting software was benefiting our competitor—not us!

The lesson: When marketing a product not considered a category leader worthy of permanent shelf space, it is necessary to work very closely with key accounts. As discussed in previous chapters, the process of planning a promotion together builds the retailer's belief in the plan and in the manufacturer. Having bought into the plan's ability to generate demand, the buyer will order sufficient quantities, and reorder and restock product throughout the promotional period.

Co-marketing, then, may be especially well suited to small manufacturing companies or those who don't possess sufficient funds to support a full-scale, new-product launch. When lacking the financial resources to invest in marketing and branding, a small business must find other ways to generate consumer demand for their product line. A primary alternative is to invest human resources into cultivating strong relationships with key retail accounts. Through these relationships, joint promotions can be developed that require no out-of-pocket expenditures. Rather than paying in cash, these promotions are paid instead through discounts on individual product orders. This form of payment encourages the retail buyer to order adequate supply of the product.

This approach has two advantages. First, it ensures that marketing funds are invested at times when there is adequate product available at retail. Second, it provides the marketing support needed to sell the product through.

This low-cost co-marketing strategy creates the same push-pull cycle between the manufacturer and retailer as its more costly cousin. It allows the manufacturer to invest in marketing and branding at a time when it matters most—when adequate product is available at retail. If successful, the marketing effort "pulls" the product through to the consumer. If the promotion proves ineffective, the buyer or merchandising manager may take an active interest in determining the cause. These individuals may even search for other ways to generate demand for the manufacturer's product.

Why would a busy buyer spend precious time seeking to promote a small company's product? There are several reasons. All are by-products of the relationship developed through the co-marketing effort.

- Since buyers don't expect automatic marketing support from small businesses like they do from larger companies, they often are willing to engage the small-company salespeople at a more human level. Buyers and merchandising personnel often empathize with employees of small and midsize businesses. Like most Americans, they enjoy rooting for the underdog.
- Secretly, some buyers wish they worked for smaller organizations where they could make a bigger splash and enjoy more freedom.
- Some buyers may take special interest in products for personal reasons (e.g., products may appeal to them or to their children).
- Some buyers may envision becoming "heroes" for recognizing the value of a new product or company before other buyers.

Since these human factors can weigh in favor of smaller businesses, every attempt must be made to find a sympathetic buyer. Sometimes, it takes just one—who is willing to trade promotional support for discounts on individual orders—to launch a product to success.

For the co-marketing strategy to work, the product's price structure must allow profitability after a 10 to 15 percent discount. This gives the salesperson the price flexibility to plan two or three promotions a year with a retail account. The retailer takes the difference between the regular and discounted price and applies it toward space in internal or external publications featuring temporary price decreases.

Without the cash to fund a branding campaign, small companies must take advantage of opportunities to work with buyers or merchandising managers on planning promotions. As these co-marketing campaigns begin to show sales results, the buyers will attach more value to this relationship. Occasionally, the manufacturer's salesperson may even move into the enviable role of a strategic vendor. A strong personal relationship can transform a coldhearted buyer into an internal champion of the product—one who takes ownership and pride in its successes.

Launching a Product from Cash Flow: The SoccerPal Story

Vidpro International, a small merchandising company located in Dallas, successfully launched a new product through key accounts on a very limited budget.

The new product took off in an airplane when Peter Stewart, Vidpro president, sat down next to a Canadian entrepreneur named Scott Vartija. The two quite naturally began talking about their children, all of whom played soccer. It turned out that the entrepreneur, Scott Vartija, had invented a soccer training device to help players practice on their own. He was looking for help to take the product to market.

The two decided to work together, using the cash flow from the original business to introduce the product to retailers. Named SoccerPal, the product was designed to sell at retail for a $6.99 to $8.99 price point, depending upon the margin needed by the particular retailer. Funds sufficient to pay for advertising and other marketing support were factored into the price structure. This factoring acknowledged the importance of building a brand franchise and generating sufficient revenue to create demand-pull promotional support.

The product was officially launched at the Super Show, America's preeminent sporting-goods trade show in Atlanta. Soccer players were hired to demonstrate the product in Vidpro's small booth. Not only did independent sporting-goods retailers show great interest, a Toys "R" Us buyer agreed to test market SoccerPal. The future looked bright.

Product was packaged and shipped to Toys "R" Us stores in the Atlanta area. Sales during the first month, however, were poor. Apparently, consumers didn't realize what the product was, so they didn't buy it. Working closely with the Toys "R" Us buyer, Vartija and Stewart planned to run a wave of local television advertising. The commercials concluded with the tag, "Available at Toys 'R' Us." This co-marketing venture involved four weeks of TV commercials, costing about $30,000.

The results were outstanding. Sell-through soared. The Toys "R" Us buyer committed to stock SoccerPal not only in its Atlanta stores, but in Toys "R" Us stores across the nation. National distribution at Toys "R" Us stores, however, was not all Vidpro executives gained for their $30,000 investment in advertising. Leveraging the successful test market in Atlanta, SoccerPal was able to gain the attention of many independent soccer and sporting-goods retailers. Distribution grew steadily.

The co-marketing approach then underwent a severe test. Wal-Mart buyers became aware of SoccerPal and offered to carry it in all their stores—with one stipulation. Wal-Mart wanted a price reduction of over a dollar a unit. The discount giant wanted to retail the product below $5. Vidpro management explained to Wal-Mart that the price reduction would eat up the margin planned for advertising and promotional support. Wal-Mart didn't budge, giving Vidpro a take-it-or-leave-it ultimatum.

Stewart and Vartija walked. They realized that without the profit margin necessary to fund marketing activity, the product would be forced to sell itself off the shelf. That condition was viewed as severely limiting. The two stood by their marketing beliefs, even though it meant saying no to America's number one retailer.

For the next two years, Vidpro personnel worked closely with key accounts including Toys "R" Us, The Sports Authority, and Oshmans, as well as over 1,500 independent sporting-goods stores. TV commercials were scheduled during peak seasons, and display space was secured whenever it became available.

Eventually, the mass merchandisers took a second look at SoccerPal. Kmart and Target tested the product, and successful tests resulted in large orders to support nationwide rollouts. Finally, Wal-Mart relented and took the product—at Vidpro's price, not Wal-Mart's!

After just three years, SoccerPal had gained distribution in over 14,000 retail stores. Brand recognition was established through targeted TV advertising and co-marketing with key retailers.

The SoccerPal story serves as a classic example of how a small company can use co-marketing not only to effectively establish a retail franchise, but also to support that franchise with timely advertising and promotional support. Working closely with key accounts to schedule timely promotions on an account-by-account basis is an effective way for the underfunded manufacturer to build a successful consumer franchise.

For Your Review

Reasons to avoid the key-account trap:

- Large accounts push hard for the lowest price. Because midsize accounts are accustomed to paying a higher price, their overall profit as a percentage of sales is usually higher, though large accounts may have the highest percentage of sales.
- Large accounts are less cooperative and more demanding. Midsize accounts are willing to partner with manufacturers to increase profits for both.
- Large accounts do not maintain full-line distribution. Midsize accounts focused on supplying a high level of customer satisfaction, however, will not only maintain full-line distribution, but will carry higher-priced and more profitable products.
- Midsize accounts are good places to test new products: the products are less likely to get knocked off by copycat manufacturers.
- Manufacturers who rely exclusively on large accounts usually regret it, as they end up forced to provide the category killer with a new product or lose the account.

Use three different approaches according to account types:

1. key-account plan—for large accounts
2. second-tier plan—for midsize accounts
3. standard co-op—for midsize and small accounts

Basically, these plans establish guidelines that treat partners according to their needs and goals, helping both them and savvy manufacturers to maximize profits.

Tips for small businesses:

- Invest human resources into cultivating strong relationships with your key accounts, especially when planning promotions or new-product launches.
- Use the transaction model to document agreements, proofs-of-performance, and payments by large accounts. You must be able to know if your promotions are working.
- Discover what motivates your large accounts' buyers. Be prepared to buy their "services"—but only if such promotions drive sales. Use your information to know which promotions are worth considering.
- If you have good relationships with your key accounts, use the low-cost marketing strategy of setting up joint promotions where your partner gets paid through discounts on product orders.
- Good relationships with your buyers will encourage them to take human interest in you, the small business, and they will invest time to help figure out how to effectively promote your product.

Remember, if your channel partners support your product, they will make sure to carry an adequate amount when you run your promotion, and everyone will profit.

PART

2 Implementing the Co-Marketing Plan

The second part of this book presents an integrated strategic approach to the development and implementation of a co-marketing plan. Each step of the eight-step process is elaborated with examples, drawn from actual co-marketing programs, to illustrate the data presented. The book now shifts from a what-and-why focus to a how-to discussion, with the hope that this information will help you to implement a co-marketing program of your own. While examples are drawn from real programs, much of the information has been changed to maintain confidentiality.

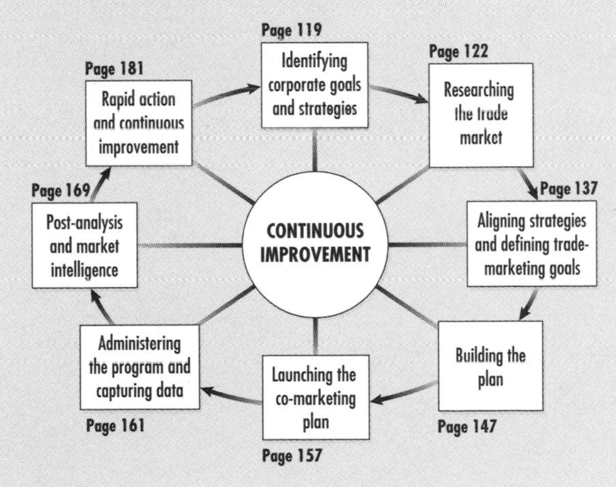

8

Determining Your Goals and Partners' Expectations for the Co-Marketing Plan

STEP 1 Identifying Corporate Goals and Strategies

The Co-Marketing Solution, much like a consumer-marketing effort, begins by identifying key corporate goals and strategies. Some companies have established clearly defined objectives. Most have not. In fact, in some companies, each executive seems to have a different set of corporate objectives. Corporate objectives must include consideration of its consumer, its products and technology, and its financial well-being.

Reviewing the direction given to the company's advertising agency can identify the consumer facet. If the company and advertising agency work according to a positioning strategy statement, the accompanying creative strategy will contain much of the necessary information about the consumer facet. Relevant information will include the target market, the unique selling proposition, the focus of sale, the product features, and the mood and tone. If a positioning strategy statement does not exist, then it is advisable to develop one. This document is detailed in Chapter 2 of this book.

To identify the financial and technological objectives, documents in addition to the positioning strategy statement should be reviewed. They include, but are not limited to the company's

- business plan
- strategic plan
- technology plan
- product plans
- research and development (R&D) plan

After those responsible for applying the Co-Marketing Solution have carefully reviewed the documents, individual meetings with key corporate executives should be arranged. Participants should include the executives responsible for developing and implementing strategy (e.g., the vice presidents of marketing, sales, finance, and strategic planning) and the directors reporting to them. These meetings should be conducted using a formal interview guide. Some questions that prove helpful in conducting meaningful interviews are

1. Where are you seeing the biggest problems facing our business right now and in the near future?
2. What are your thoughts and observations, given our overall corporate strategy (reference specific strategies), and how does it impact your operating department?
3. What departmental strategies have you developed to deliver our company goal?
4. What tactics are you employing to deliver them?
5. How are you allocating your budget? What percentage of funds are you spending against the strategies mentioned?
6. How does our relationship with the trade impact your department?
7. What are your thoughts concerning our co-op policies?
8. In an ideal world, what would you like to see us doing with our co-op and trade marketing funds?
9. Are there any trade accounts that especially concern you? For what reason?

At these meetings, the co-marketing team should share their research and analysis of the company documents, as well as their preliminary conclusions on the corporate objectives. Feedback from key executives will lead to additions, deletions, and modifications. This process will distill the key issues of the organization (including personal initiatives of top executives). The resulting series of brief statements should capture the overall strategic goals of the company.

The following are the strategic goals at a wireless communications company where I facilitated the creation of a co-marketing plan during the late 1990s.

1. **Grow at the market rate or greater.**
   This objective was included because it was deemed important to show Wall Street analysts that the company was maintaining market share. The rate of customer growth would be sufficient to keep the stock price up.

2. **Skew spending toward adding and keeping the more profitable customers.**
   This objective took into account the cost of adding a customer, which was almost $400 in marketing expense and unabsorbed telephone cost. Low-usage customers were worth just $35 a month in service revenue. Having too large a proportion of low-usage customers could seriously impact profit margins.

3. **Create maximum value for exclusive channel partners.**
   This objective recognized a competitive environment in which many exclusive agents (who each carried only one wireless service) were being asked to consider adding PCS (personal communication services) phones and service to their product lines. It was deemed essential to give these agents reasons to maintain exclusivity and to develop a plan to compete effectively with agents who became nonexclusive.

4. **Establish a national brand image.**
   Overall category spending had increased exponentially, making it more and more difficult to maintain advertising share of voice (SOV). Consolidating all marketing activity behind a consistent brand message was deemed essential to deriving the most bang for the marketing buck. Sharpening the marketing message to

communicate a consistent brand image was also considered essential.

Finally, after conducting these interviews with key managers, it is important to document findings. It is helpful to do this in concise statements that identify the goals of the organization, as was illustrated in the preceding example. It is also important to identify strategies and tactics that may conflict with one another. Pointing these out in a nonjudgmental way helps gain maximum value. For example, a statement could be "The marketing goal of focused spending is not being consistently followed in the regional and indirect channels and should be reviewed."

Once the corporate goals and strategies have been identified, it's time to move to the second step of the Co-Marketing Solution: Using market research to bench-mark the trade environment and the impact of current spending upon the sales force and the trade partners.

STEP 2 Researching the Trade Market

Quantitative and qualitative research will reveal benchmarks on co-op spending and its performance. But it also produces a valuable by-product. The time researchers spend listening to customers and skilled salespeople generates something more than just data. By talking to researchers, customers and salespeople become participants in the eventual plan. They will be eager to see whether their input was used. Their input virtually guarantees that they will be inclined to buy into the eventual program. This buy-in improves the program's chances for success, because the salespeople and customers will play key roles in it.

Just the by-product of market research makes it worthwhile. Yet in virtually every business, administrators and salespeople are tempted to skip this step. "We don't need to research our program. We talk to our customers every day," say administrators and salespeople. "They will just say . . . " At this point, the administrators and salespeople string together their personal beliefs. Often, they insist that customers, usually the big ones, want more money and fewer hassles about how to spend it. The comments by administrators usually imply adversarial relationships with their customers.

They also reveal the administrators to be good people who don't understand why they are constantly under attack. What they fail to realize is that customer complaining does not reflect at all on their job performance. The complaining is posturing and simply a negotiating ploy—similar to the way a football coach works the referee after a disputed call. The coach (customer) expects that on the next questionable call, the referee (administrator) will give his team the break. Even when the football coach may not totally disagree with a referee's call, he will nevertheless plead his team's case. Likewise, customers can rarely be considered unbiased.

Administrators often succumb to the "squeaky wheel effect." Since much of their job consists of dealing with dissatisfied customers (or ones feigning dissatisfaction), the administrator may feel that few satisfied customers exist. As in most businesses, happy customers rarely call or write. Thus, the administrator's view is understandably skewed.

Typically, valid research paints a very different picture from that of the administrator. It is a rather simple matter to ensure that customers respond without bias: researchers conceal the identity of the manufacturer conducting the study. This "blind taste test" technique gathers unbiased perceptions about each manufacturer within the category and rates them against one another. This information can be very different from the feedback the salesperson receives from a customer who attempts to exert some leverage to negotiate for more funds, better pricing, or product-return authorizations. This blind-survey technique produces a true evaluation of how the company's program compares to other programs, indicating its position in relation to its competitors.

To transform the strategies identified in Step 1 into an effective co-marketing program, your competitive position must be researched and understood.

Market research should shed light on

1. the customers' (i.e., trade partners') wants, needs, and attitudes
2. the salespeople's points of view
3. the competitive landscape and your company's position within it

Attitude, Awareness & Usage (AA&U) Research

It is very important to accurately measure the wants, needs, and attitudes of your channel partners. I strongly recommend using trained interviewers to conduct telephone interviews. This methodology is more expensive than mail- or fax-back surveys, but it is well worth the extra cost. Mail and fax back do not guarantee inclusion of the real target you're after. Response rates are low and the most important and busiest people rarely have time to participate. Also, these methodologies tend to skew results because they don't allow a trained interviewer to probe for complete answers and obtain a complete interview. Field the research using a blind format; i.e., ask participants to answer the questions, without telling them which company is fielding the research.

Conduct this quantitative study among all major accounts using a sample size of at least 50 customers from each channel. This provides a sufficient sample to analyze and compare data from: large customers, average-sized customers, national accounts, wholesale distributors, etc. In this way you can compare how the needs and attitudes of each different, homogeneous segment of your overall channel rate differ. This is very important. A common mistake made by many companies is to assume that all of their channel partners have the same problems and desires.

The target for this research is the key contact at the trade partner for co-op. This might be a buyer, a merchandising manager, or sometimes, a senior administrator; it differs by account, but it is always the person who works with most of the co-op claimed and spent within the category. The researcher interviews the account's point person on co-op programs by phone using a standard questionnaire. The questionnaire gathers information on six issues:

1. awareness of all manufacturers' plans and programs
2. ratings of those plans and programs
3. attitudes and reasons about liking or disliking programs
4. how co-op funds are used
5. ideas for better use of those funds
6. relative generosity and effectiveness of different manufacturers' plans and programs

Desktop Software Questionnaire

Account name: ______________________ Interviewer: ______________________

Person interviewed: ______________________ Title: ______________________

Classification: ☐ VAR (value-added reseller) ☐ Distributor ☐ National Account ☐ Retailer

Type of VAR: ☐ Accounting/Finance ☐ Graphics ☐ Document

(Confirm that the person you're talking with is the contact for co-op and promotional funds, or is in charge of co-op administration.)

Hello, my name is ________ with TradeOne Marketing, a co-op and trade promotion firm located in Texas. One of your software publishers gave us your name and asked us to talk to you to find out what you think about promotional and co-op funds and any ideas you might have. This information will help this publisher design trade promotion programs that work better. I have been asked not to identify who the publisher is until the end of the interview. What we want is your most honest opinions about promotional funds, both good and bad, so that our publisher can use their funds more effectively to help you build your sales.

Would you mind answering a few questions for me? It will take about five minutes of your time, and the information you give will be kept strictly confidential and only revealed to the client as part of the total. No salesperson will call on you as a result of this research.

To begin, I'd like to ask you some questions about promotional funds in general.

1. When I mention promotion or co-op, which manufacturers' programs immediately come to mind?
2. (Check names and circle the first name mentioned. Confirm that these are all the programs that come to the contact's mind.)

   On a scale of 1 to 10, with 10 being best, how would you rate your overall feeling about each of the programs you just mentioned. (Read names and place rating after each name.)
3. Rating

Rating	Reimbursement %	Requirements
Software Co. A ________	________	________
Software Co. B ________	________	________
Software Co. C ________	________	________
Software Co. D ________	________	________
Software Co. E ________	________	________
Other ________	________	________

4. Could you summarize what you especially like about the programs you rate highly? ______________
5. Could you also summarize what you dislike about some programs that leads you to not think highly of them?

   ____
6. Which software publisher has the best promotional support program? ______________________
7. Why is their program so good? ______________________________

8. If you were going to design a promotional allowance program that was just perfect for your company, what guidelines would it contain? ____________________

____

____

9. Using 10 for extremely important and 1 for not important at all, how would you rate each of the following program options?

a. TV advertising ________
b. radio advertising ________
c. direct mail ________
d. newspaper advertising ________
e. Yellow Pages advertising ________
f. displays or certification plaques ________
g. advertising help designing ads and mailers ________
h. sales bonus or spiffs ________
i. mystery shopper rewards ________
j. frequent buyer program ________
k. sales leads ________
l. manufacturer's help with using their promotional funds ________

Now I'd like to ask you to rate a couple of specific desktop software promotional programs. Use 10 for excellent and 1 for poor.

10. How do you rate Software Co. A's program? _______ Why? ____________________
11. Would you say Software Co. A's program is: ☐ more or ☐ less generous than most other programs? (☐ don't know)
12. Is it easy to understand? ☐ yes ☐ no (☐ don't know about it ☐ don't understand it)
13. Is it easy to get paid? ☐ yes ☐ no
14. Is it well-thought-out when compared to other co-op programs in general? ☐ yes ☐ no
15. How do you rate Software Co. B's program? __________ Why? ____________________
16. Would you say the Software Co. B's program is: ☐ more or ☐ less generous than most other programs? (☐ don't know)
17. Is it easy to understand? ☐ yes ☐ no (☐ don't know about it ☐ don't understand it)
18. Is it easy to get paid? ☐ yes ☐ no
19. Is it well-thought-out when compared to other co-op programs in general? ☐ yes ☐ no
20. Is there any advice that you would like to give management at [your company] about how to make their promotional program more effective? ☐ no ☐ yes If yes, what? ____________________

The wording of questions is important and should be pretested to ensure that respondents understand the questions and are providing answers consistent with all the pertinent information. This sample questionnaire contains many of the standard questions typically found useful in this type of research.

Thank them for their time. If they ask, reveal that your company is the manufacturer and that this information will be used to help your company assess the effectiveness of their promotional program.

Analyzing Results

After the fieldwork is completed, it is time to create master tables and analyze the data. I use The Survey System, one of many software packages into which you can input data and create data tables and graphs. Whichever package you use, the desired results are data tables that show the significant relationships. These tables should be formatted as follows:

Question 1

Observations:

Total	Key Accounts	Second Tier Accounts	Small Accounts	Individual Channels

Question 2

Observations:

Total	Key Accounts	Second Tier Accounts	Small Accounts	Individual Channels

After all of the questions have been filled into the data tables, which are then analyzed for pertinent observations, it is time to write an executive summary. The summary presents

- a brief summary of the reason the research was fielded
- the methodology used
- key findings
- appropriate conclusions
- recommended action

The overall perspective gained from this research can then be shared appropriately during field visits to "compare notes" and probe for what is happening behind the numbers.

Field Immersion

For researchers, there is no better way to understand what salespeople experience on a daily basis than to spend some time with them making calls. Field immersion gives researchers this chance to walk in salespeople's shoes and to sit in on meetings with a few customers.

Two important objectives are accomplished by spending "windshield" time—in the car between calls—with salespeople. First, this time provides the opportunity to discuss results of the AA&U survey. Salespeople's opinions on and insights into this data can be invaluable. Second, windshield time reinforces for salespeople the credibility of the research and the programs developed from that research. Since the salespeople will be the chief implementers of the program, it is crucial that they buy into the research process.

It's a good strategy to spend time with the most influential salespeople. Their buy-in can lead the rest of the sales force to do the same. They'll be more likely to take ownership of the programs when they know the programs have been developed to address the problems they face daily. The following is a generic communication guide to illustrate the kind of questions you'll want to ask during these informal interviews.

Key customers should also be interviewed for the same reasons salespeople were interviewed—to gain perspective about the survey research and to create buy-in from key users of the program. Working with customers, especially difficult ones, provides valuable insight into the problems likely to occur during program implementation. Assessing customers' needs and desires will ensure that the right amount of quid pro quo is built into the program. It also provides a

Sample Field Interview Discussion Guide

How do you rate the current co-op program?______________________________

What is good about it?

____

____

What needs improving?

____

____

What are the major challenges you're facing with accounts?

____

____

____

____

____

How could co-op help resolve these problems?

____

____

____

____

____

What information would you like to have about your accounts?

____

____

____

____

What problems will we face if we change the current program?

____

____

____

What would you like to see a revised program include?

____

____

____

____

What should we avoid when changing the program?

____

____

____

____

____

chance to begin preselling some of the strategies and recommendations suggested by the AA&U study. This assessment can provide invaluable learning and insight regarding the trade's perspective on what you might be considering.

Remember the goal is to pull key customers into the planning process to co-develop a marketing program that advances both corporate and customer objectives. Avoid trying to impose objectives on customers that are contrary to their goals.

Often, some of the real problem accounts are the quickest to respond to the manufacturer's change in attitude. An example of how one manufacturer won over Best Buy by using this attitude of cooperation is reviewed in Chapter 6.

Review of Competitive Programs

During the survey research, the category's various programs are bench-marked by compiling customers' responses. Now researchers review actual program guidelines to determine what each competitor is offering the customer. This review process includes the program documents that are presented to the customer. Program guidelines outline the program for the customer. These limited-circulation documents are issued directly from the manufacturer to its trade partners.

How does one obtain these documents? The first place to start is a publication called *Co-op Programs Sourcebook*, which lists many of the published guidelines that retailers, distributors, and ad agencies use. This sourcebook is available from National Register Publishing and can be ordered by calling (908) 464-6800.

Unfortunately, many of the programs' guidelines are not available in this sourcebook. Salespeople may be able to obtain such documents from customers with whom they enjoy good relations. Also, during the market research phase, some customers during the interview will agree to mail or fax copies of guidelines if asked by the interviewer. It's also a good idea to post guidelines on a Website for easy downloading.

Once the guidelines and terms have been gathered, it is helpful to create a spreadsheet comparing the pertinent features of each manufacturer's program. Table 8.1 illustrates a group of competitive programs in the wireless phone category:

TABLE 8.1 Competitive Program Matrix

Manufacturer	Accrual	Reimbursement	Availability	Prior Approval Required?	Check or Cash Reimbursement?	Timing	Eligible Media
Phone Maker A Cellular	1.25% on phones (1% of this for general use, .25% for lit and displays) 1% on accessories	25% for nonexclusive 50% for exclusive 75% for either a Phone Maker A–produced ad or a carrier-produced ad featuring Signature brand 100% for Phone Maker A–produced Signature brand ads	Dealers	All customer-produced ads, not required on manufacturer-produced ads	Credit memo	Calendar year accrual Accounts have until 3/31 to submit claims Monthly accruals	Newspaper Yellow Pages Outdoor Radio/TV Brochures/Direct Mail POP Posters/Banners Internet Literature Ad specialty
Phone Maker B Mass Retailer Program	2% of purchases	50%	Mass Retailers	All customer-produced ads, not required on manufacturer-produced ads	Check	Calendar year accrual Have until 2/28 to submit Monthly accruals	Same as above, plus: catalog, cable TV
Phone Maker B Dealer Program	3% of purchases	50%	Dealers	All customer-produced ads, not required on manufacturer-produced ads	Check	Calendar year accrual Have until 2/28 to submit Monthly accruals	Same as above, plus: catalog, cable TV
Phone Maker C	2% of purchases	50%	Dealers	All customer-produced ads, not required on manufacturer-produced ads Products must be illustrated	Credit memo	12-month program with quarterly accruals Have until 2/28 to submit	Same as above

TABLE 8.1 Competitive Program Matrix (continued)

Manufacturer	Accrual	Reimbursement	Availability	Prior Approval Required	Check or Cash Reimbursement	Timing	Eligible Media
Phone Maker D Dealer Program	3% of purchases	100%	Dealers	All customer-produced, ads not required on manufacturer-produced ads	DFI	Annual rolling, accounts have 180 days to spend accruals, and 30 days to submit claims	Same as above, plus: catalog, direct mail, demonstrator, exhibits
Phone Maker D Retailer Program	Negotiated with each account	100%	Retailers	Yes, products must be illustrated	Credit memo	Annual rolling, accounts have 180 days to spend accruals, and 30 days to submit claims	Radio/TV Newspaper Inserts Weekly newspaper Magazine Outdoor Yellow Pages Cable TV
Phone Maker E	2% of purchases	100%	Retailers	Prior approval required for all media	Credit memo	Accruals from 4/1–3/31 claims due by 5/15	TV/Radio Newspaper Weekly newspaper Magazine Outdoor Signs

TABLE 8.1 Competitive Program Matrix (continued)

Manufacturer	Accrual	Reimbursement	Availability	Prior Approval Required	Check or Cash Reimbursement	Timing	Eligible Media
Phone Maker F	1–2% depending on account	60–100%	Dealers	Prior approval required for all media, except manufacturer-produced ads	Check	Accruals from 10/1–9/30 claims due by 2/15	TV/Radio Newspaper Weekly newspaper Magazine Outdoor Signs
Phone Maker A Pagers	2%	50% on dealer-created media 75% for Phone Maker A benefit copy 100% for Phone Maker A–produced 10% for exhibit booth space	Dealers	Prior approval required for all media, except manufacturer-produced ads	Check	1/1–12/31 5/31 to submit claims	TV/Radio Print Yellow Pages Direct mail Customer-produced promos Literature/Collateral Internet Trade shows
Phone Carrier A	Negotiated on account-by-account basis	50%	Authorized retailers	Yes	Check	Monthly accruals that roll off after 120 days 90 days to submit claims	Newspaper Magazines Direct mail Literature Radio/TV Displays Ad specialty
Phone Carrier B	$25 per activation	50%	Authorized agents	Yes	Check	Monthly accruals that	Newspaper Magazines

TABLE 8.1 Competitive Program Matrix

Manufacturer	Accrual	Reimbursement	Availability	Prior Approval Required	Check or Cash Reimbursement	Timing	Eligible Media
						roll off after 6 months 90 days to submit claims	Direct mail Literature Radio/TV Displays Ad specialty Telemarketing
Phone Carrier C	$30 per activation, 2% of which can be used for ad specialty	50%	Authorized agents/ dealers/ retailers	Yes	Check	Monthly accruals that roll off after 12 months 90 days to submit claims	Newspaper Magazines Direct mail Literature Radio/TV Displays Ad specialty Telemarketing
Phone Carrier D	$50 per activation	75%	Authorized agents/ dealers/ retailers	Yes	Check	Monthly accruals that roll off after 12 months	Same as Phone Carrier C
Phone Carrier E	$25 per activation	75% for all qualified expenditures 100% for Ameritech-created ads, ads combining paging and cellular	Authorized dealers	Yes	Check	Monthly accruals that roll off after 6 months 60 days to submit claims	Newspaper Magazines Radio/TV Direct mail Outdoor Yellow Pages

Table 8.1 shows the types of information obtained from auditing customer claims.

Armed with this market research, it is time to align strategies and define trade-marketing goals.

For Your Review

Step 1: Identifying Corporate Goals and Strategies

Review key corporate documents:

- Make sure your company has a positioning strategy statement.
- Look over your company's marketing, strategic, business, technology, and research and development plans.

Conduct personal interviews with key executives in your company:

- Explore each department's tactics to deliver corporate strategy.
- Determine attitudes and needs regarding trade partners.

Document findings from personal interviews:

- Draw up concise statements that identify your company's goals.
- Diplomatically bring conflicting strategies and tactics to management's attention.

Step 2: Researching the Trade Market

Forward-looking companies take the time to research their trade market because

- They discover benchmarks on co-op spending and performance.
- By talking to customers and salespeople, the company generates commitment to the plan. The support of customers and salespeople in their key roles will improve the program.

When you use the AA&U telephone survey to measure the wants and perceptions of your channel partners, keep in mind these points:

- Interview at least 50 dealers per channel.
- Develop a standard questionnaire.
- Conduct interviews blind to get unbiased ratings.
- Talk to as many large dealers as possible.
- Don't assume that all dealers have similar needs.
- Determine their ratings of other co-op programs.
- Pinpoint their reasons for liking or disliking particular co-op programs.
- Find out how co-op funds are currently spent.
- Get ideas for better use of funds.
- Compare relative generosity and effectiveness of different manufacturers' programs.

Be sure to spend time in the field working with top salespeople and visiting key accounts:

- Gain their opinions and insights concerning the results of the AA&U surveys.
- Establish credibility with them concerning the research and the programs resulting from the research.
- Get buy-in for future recommendations.
- Identify potential problems in implementation.
- Take the time to determine what your competitors are doing and how effective their programs are.
- Recall the blind ratings per channel gathered from the AA&U study.
- Gather formal program guidelines and develop a competitive matrix.

9

Setting Up Your Co-Marketing Plan

STEP 3 Aligning Strategies and Defining Trade-Marketing Goals

In the first two steps of the Co-Marketing Solution, four important ingredients of the trade-marketing component have been identified:

1. the key corporate goals and strategies
2. the current spending patterns
3. the relationship of these patterns to the marketing messages presented to consumers
4. an evaluation of the current program compared to competitors' programs and trade partners' desires

Now it is time to develop trade-marketing objectives and the means by which those objectives will be measured. Before formulating these goals, it is helpful to consider what marketing messages, from all sources, are being delivered to potential consumers and what the company's distribution will look like in a mature market.

Once the brief statements of corporate objectives have been developed, the next step is to take a look at the marketing message being presented to the end user. Does the message being presented to the consumer correspond with these corporate objectives?

Monitoring the Marketing Messages

As the co-marketing team reviews the brand messages consumers receive, it is helpful to back up and assess the big picture. The total amount of market spending should be calculated. The people who have control over that spending should be identified. Further, the avenues through which marketing messages reach consumers should be outlined. The results of such an assessment is often eye-opening for those who had no concept of the size of the trade-marketing program.

Once executives become aware that the trade-marketing budget is as large or larger than the consumer-marketing budget, they are more likely to consider the reengineering of their trade-marketing program. Often, the trade-marketing budget dwarfs the consumer-marketing budget by two or three times, making the argument even more convincing.

Figure 9.1 presents an overview of such an analysis. When viewed in its entirety, this analysis revealed many new things about how this leading telecommunications service provider was spend-

FIGURE 9.1 Co-Op, Market Spending Overview

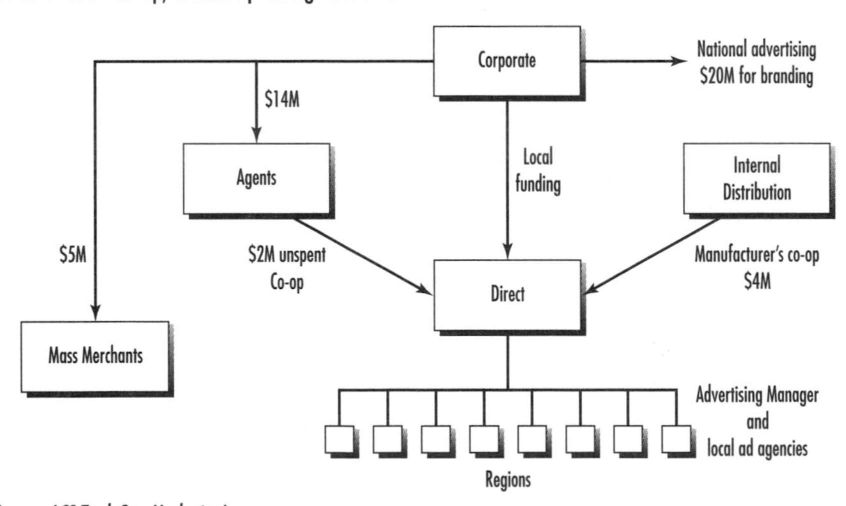

(Source: ACS TradeOne Marketing)

Figure 9.1 describes the source of marketing messages for a company involved in the wireless phone service category, the dollars spent at each level, and who controls the consumer message.

ing their money. These were facts that most executives knew, but which had not been viewed in the big-picture form and as such were quite startling. Bench-marking revealed that

- About $20 million was spent nationally by the corporate marketing department with the help of the ad agency.
- Another $6 million was spent by the marketing and advertising managers in each region. These people had their own separate advertising agencies and developed their own creative strategies without corporate direction.
- $14 million was spent by small retail agents through the co-op budget.
- Finally, $5 million was spent by mass merchants.

Surprisingly, all but the national messaging was being developed without knowledge of the corporate strategic direction!

TradeOne Marketing found that over one-half of the advertising spending was being developed by the regional offices or their retailers. This percentage is not unusually high. These messages were not being managed with anything resembling a consistent strategy. In fact, most of these messages were not being monitored at all. Worse yet, the corporate strategy was not even available to those trade partners who sought it.

As disconnected as this situation appears, it is not extraordinary. It is, in fact, fairly common. Not only does it run the risk of eroding the brand message, but it also wastes valuable marketing dollars. And that may be small potatoes compared to the impact on the consumer.

The many discordant messages confuse the consumer. With so many companies confusing so many consumers, it's no wonder that most products lack clear positions in the public's mind. Even market leaders are vulnerable when they send confusing, even contradictory, messages to the consumer. They may own the shelf, but they do not own a permanent position within the collective mind of the consumer.

Conversely, well-positioned market leaders own a piece of the consumer consciousness. Think of McDonald's or Coca-Cola. Regardless of whether a person likes these products, the perception and knowledge the person has of them are universally communicated with a commonly understood message. A clear product positioning has been established.

In today's cluttered marketplace, with many competitors vying for the prospective consumer's attention, it is critical to focus your marketing message and spending. To allow the brand message to be eroded by unmanaged trade spending should be avoided at all costs. Analyzing the big picture helps prevent your company from falling prey to this silent killer of the brand message.

Distribution in a Mature Market

To create a long-lasting plan that will minimize channel conflict, the co-marketing team must look into the future to project and define the product line's marketplace at maturity. This will encourage the team to examine the role of each possible distribution channel as the market matures.

By defining the marketplace at maturity, a long-term, integrated approach to channel management becomes possible. Many companies develop a plan without considering the possibility of a new class of distribution down the road. When that change becomes a reality, conflicts often arise among some of the older, valued distribution channels. This scenario occurs frequently when a product distributed only in specialty retailers is suddenly added to the shelves of the large mass merchants. If not planned for, the smaller retailer tends to feel betrayed and will inevitably drop the product, sometimes dropping the manufacturer. Such is the level of animosity between specialty and "big box" retailers. To prevent future channel conflict, planners must, therefore, establish up front the role and importance of each channel in the distribution mix over the maturation of the market. Full maturity is defined as that time when the product is selling profitably at its maximum number of outlets. (Profitability here applies to the reseller.) Dealers, distributors, mass merchants, specialty retailers, catalogs, and the Internet should be among the channels considered.

A plan that clarifies the roles of existing and potential distribution channels will maximize the value of each channel. In this way, a harmonious approach to distribution can be devised. If your individual distribution strategies are designed with an appreciation of the market at maturity, an overall harmonious distribution strategy can be designed that will work in the short as well as the long term. This careful planning will minimize any future channel conflicts. While the role of one distribution channel might be to obtain new customers, the role of another channel might be to maintain old customers; the role of a third might be to provide product service.

The plan should outline for the channel partners how they are expected to promote the product and how they are protected from members of other distribution channels. In this way, the manufacturer ensures that each channel partner understands their role in promoting the product. Developing specific guidelines will be discussed later in this book.

Many traditional cellular phone carriers faced the challenge of managing distribution in a rapidly changing marketplace in the 1990s. The following case illustrates the importance of identifying and orchestrating the roles of channel partners to maximize sales and profit.

The advent of PCS phones—offered by global carriers such as Sprint PCS—created havoc in the traditional cellular market in 1996. This market had evolved as an oligopoly because FCC licenses protected purchasers within geographically limited areas. PCS phones sold through electronic retailers were changing this secure distribution arrangement. All of a sudden, service was being offered through national companies such as Sprint PCS and PrimeCo, and their products retailed nationally at stores like Radio Shack.

This development begged the question, "Where will end users buy wireless phones and phone service in a mature marketplace?" To answer this question, strategists developed a distribution and service matrix chart (Figure 9.2).

On one axis, the destination versus nondestination purchases were plotted. On the other axis, the importance of wireless phones to the retailer was plotted (i.e., is the retailer's operation focused around wireless phones, or is it just an occasional retailer of these products?).

The analysis helped pinpoint the role each type of channel partner might play in a mature marketplace. Pinpointing these roles helped define the appropriate strategic goals for each channel. Four findings emerged:

FIGURE 9.2 Distribution/Service Matrix

	Nonexclusive	Exclusive
Destination Purchase	Electronic Retailers Need: ▲ priority placement ▲ sales incentives ▲ pay for performance ▲ training	High-Touch/Service ▲ co-stores ▲ specialty stores (dedicated to cellular) Need: ▲ upgrade, retention programs ▲ depth of sale training/products
Non-destination Purchase	Mass Merchants Need: ▲ in/out, seasonal promotions ▲ hot offers that drive turn	Department Stores/Rural Retailers

(Source: ACS TradeOne Marketing)

Figure 9.2 classifies retailers by the focus they have on the product category, their ability to deliver service, and the competitive environment at the shelf level.

1. Specialty stores will play the role of delivering high levels of service and selection. This role will be especially helpful to the more experienced buyer who appreciates the differences in available products. Many of these retailers will remain loyal to one service provider.
2. Chain electronic stores will deliver high levels of service and selection. But they will also feature many competitive products; so it is necessary to compete at the shelf level in these stores.
3. National mass merchants will offer tremendous retail exposure. But they will expect low pricing and high retail turnover. They will have difficulty offering any customer service, so the product must be able to sell itself.
4. Nonexclusive, low-service retailers, such as department stores, will have trouble competing long-term. They will expect higher profit margins than the mass merchants and have some of the same problems offering customer service.

Upon assessing the strengths and limitations of each of these channels, two conclusions were reached. First, the service-oriented channels should be used to cater to sophisticated and service-oriented customers. Second, the mass channels should be used to attract first-time users with best-price offers and low-feature products. Figure 9.3 illustrates the role that each of the surviving channels in the wireless market might play in a balanced distribution approach to the market.

It is very important to think through what distribution might look like two to five years down the road to determine exactly what each channel can best contribute to your goals. After all, the goal is to have your product available when and where consumers are willing to buy it, and in the form that is best suited for that purchase occasion. Taking a forward look at the future shape of your marketplace is a strategic exercise that can reduce the risk of unwanted channel conflict later. It also helps clarify exactly why you are dealing with each type of channel partner and what you should expect from them.

Co-Marketing Goals and Measurement Techniques

The trade area provides many new areas of measurement that benefit both the channel spending analysis and the consumer marketplace. Since the final result of trade marketing is sell-through to the end user, co-marketing can yield valuable insight into the delivery of the overall marketing strategy. Careful planning to set appropriate goals for the co-marketing plan must be developed along with the tools to measure those goals.

FIGURE 9.3 Channel Roles at Maturity

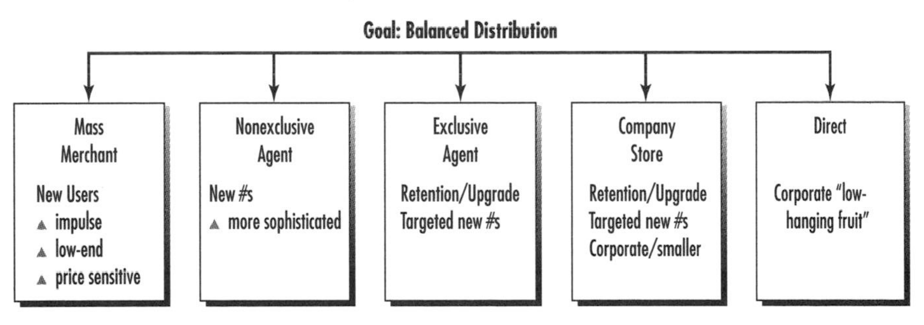

(Source: ACS TradeOne Marketing)

Figure 9.3 describes the role each distribution channel will play when the market is at full maturity and the potential manner in which each channel should be used to attract or retain customers.

Some co-marketing goals and the techniques for measuring them include:

- **Sales:**
  A baseline for measuring sales is established (i.e., sales figures before implementation of the program). These baseline figures are then compared with the figures produced during the lifetime of the program. Pre- and post-program sales figures can be taken on an account-by-account basis.

  Sales by those customers who use the program to its fullest—identified by their higher reimbursement rates—can be compared with sales by those customers who make more modest use of the program. Make sure you can track the growth rate of each account in sales. This will allow you to compare the fast-growth accounts and how they are spending their co-op funds, with how average- and low-growth accounts are using theirs.

- **Media weight:**
  Advertising can be tracked in two ways: the dollar value and the percentage of advertising that includes desired branding messages. Both can be compared with baseline figures to determine whether overall category spending is trending up or down.

- **Program usage:**
  There should be two goals against which claims are measured: the desired percentage of available funds to be claimed and the desired amount of spending in accordance with the preferred strategy. Throughout the program, these percentages and spending figures produce valuable feedback.

- **Customer satisfaction:**
  Customer satisfaction ratings can be obtained using regularly scheduled AA&U studies to continue bench-marking the effectiveness of the program. These studies should be performed at least annually, preferably every six months.

- **Sales force satisfaction:**
  Sales force satisfaction can be measured on a regular basis. Research questionnaires should be filled out annually.

- **Logo guideline adherence:**
  All ads on record should be checked for possible misuse of trademarks or of minimum-advertised-price (MAP) guidelines.

- **Market data:**
  Copy point delivery, branding communication, price points, share of voice, share of promotional space, etc., are captured and analyzed. This analysis provides the basic data required to track ROI analysis of promotions and spending programs.

An Example of Measuring Program Effectiveness

The following example of program measurement techniques comes from the wireless telephone service marketplace. Note the specificity with which co-marketing goals can be set and measured.

Reporting on the following measures will aid in gauging the success of the program:

1. **Funds usage**
   a. Are funds being spent? And to what degree by channel?
   b. Measure to show what percentage of available funds is actually being used.
2. **Effectiveness**
   a. Are funds being spent the way the manufacturer wants?
   b. Is participant advertising communicating the regional copy goals?
   c. Do ads contain the appropriate legal copy?
   d. Measure percentage of ads containing each.
3. **Results**
   a. Identify how the fast-growth agents spend their money and what types of ads they produce and place.
   b. By measuring the growth of those agents spending correctly versus those not spending correctly, or not spending at all, and correlating the spending back to growth and retention, the manufacturer can skew spending toward fast-growth marketing efforts.
   c. Measure the relative cost of adding each activation during different promotions.

4. **Marketing Intelligence**
   a. Measure the manufacturer's share of local market advertising and what consumer messages are being delivered.
   b. Track competitive offers and report them to management.
   c. Calculate ROI and market effectiveness ratings.

The redesigned program should:

▲ Create accurate, timely payment and reporting of all claims, limiting the strategic risk of having different programs and payment policies in place should the manufacturer be challenged legally.

▲ Provide a higher level of customer satisfaction:

Customer Service Ratings

Current vs. Goal (1: lowest, 10: highest)

	Current	Goal
Guidelines	7.4	8.0
Flexibility	7.3	7.5
Planning	3.4	7.0
Account Manager	8.5	8.5
Quick Payment	6.6	8.5
Ease of Claiming	6.6	8.5
Reimbursement	6.6	7.5

Measurement: Perform AA&U research every six months

▲ Provide market data that would improve spending effectiveness:

Goal: Skew spending toward proved, high-return events: 30 percent in year 1, 50 percent in year 2, 70 percent in year 3.

Measurement: Track the percentage of the indirect co-op budget spent against high-return events, which initially will be full-message ads, and promotions-in-a-box items. As additional high-return activities (ROI measurements, etc.) are identified, spending will be skewed toward these successful efforts as well.

▲ Provide incremental, higher-value customer additions:

Goal: Show an incremental 15 percent annual rate of acquiring new customers by agents who spend marketing funds in the recommended manner.

Measurement: Analyze effectiveness of agents who spend according to recommendations versus those who do not, and calculate the incremental new customers added based on spending patterns.

- Extend the national branding effort into local agent advertising:

  Goal: 75 percent of agent ads include consistent branding message(s).

  Measurement: Record the percentage of agent ads that contain branding copy.

- Provide incremental media weight for the money spent:

  Goal: Supplement the budget agents use to purchase advertising space by 15 percent.

  Measurement: Compare agent rates to the third-party audit firm's proprietary database of media rates to help agents learn to buy smartly and get more ad space for their money.

Once a set of goals and the measurement criteria have been established, it is time to consider the different types of trade-marketing tactics suitable to making your goals become a reality.

STEP 4 Building the Plan

Now that the groundwork has been laid, you can construct the co-marketing plan. Start by identifying the tactical programs that will contribute toward your trade-marketing goals. There are a variety of tactical programs to choose from, including:

- **Cooperative advertising:**
  Share the cost of advertising using standardized spending and reimbursement guidelines. Co-op advertising is normally used for promotion at the local market level, and this tactic is

especially effective at building consumer awareness of product availability or of a sale price.

- **Market development funds:**
These promotional funds are spent according to a plan or an agreement designed to help channel partners meet a specific strategic goal. Market development funds are also called business development funds, referring to their use on an ad hoc basis to fund activity directly tied to increased business. Quite often, these funds are used to buy back existing inventory of competitive products to create shelf space. These funds also may be used to pay for shelf fixtures that result in increased distribution.

- **Key-account planning:**
Specific plans for each major account are developed. A formal planning and approval process is used. Key-account planning seeks to match strategies with large accounts on a case-by-case basis.

- **Rebate program:**
A type of manufacturer discount that is automatically paid at the end of a given period. The amount of the rebate is based on sales. Many times, rebate programs are used in lieu of a price discount. The objective is to tie an account into a specific goal, such as a milestone based on sales.

- **Sales Person Incentive Funds (SPIF):**
Salespeople are paid funds directly based on sales performance. Sales promotion programs are used to promote sell-through and to turn the attention of the people who can make the sale toward the product. Because sales promotions are based on sales results, they are useful for identifying the most effective salespeople. One manufacturer organized a group retreat for top-performing salespeople who had been identified this way. The retreat served as a reward for the salespeople and also as an opportunity for the manufacturing team to spend additional time influencing these salespeople.

- **In-store materials and verification:**
Marketing materials are provided to the retailers. The availability of these materials can be coordinated with consumer pro-

motional offers to yield an additive effect on sales. Remember though, many manufacturers produce product literature and displays that are never used. Often, these materials never leave the back room until they are thrown out. A verification plan is a must for this tactic. Having the right materials in-store and at the point of sale (POS) to support the rest of the consumer offer creates a one-two punch that completes the message to the consumer.

- **End-user coupons and rebates:**
  Deliver promotional offers at the POS to generate product sell-through. Special offers, such as mail-in rebates, entice the end user. Rebates are less expensive than store-paid coupons because some consumers forget to return the rebate form.

- **Customer loyalty programs:**
  Often called frequent-buyer programs, these customer loyalty campaigns reward and encourage additional purchases.

- **Customer certification:**
  Customers are classified by the training they have acquired. Training is assumed to indicate an ability to deliver service. Customer certification programs are most useful for technical markets.

- **Warranty registration:**
  A database is developed to track customers according to the product purchased. Warranty registration can provide valuable marketing lists for use in product introductions, product upgrades, or accessory sales. Lists generated from warranty registrations can also be provided to channel partners for their follow-up programs.

- **Promotions-in-a-box:**
  Prepackaged promotions are customized for use in the retailer's trading area. Activities often included in these programs (e.g., direct mail, telemarketing, and POS displays) can be very effective in reaching a local market. Promotions-in-a-box are especially appropriate for midsize to small retailers who do not have the manpower to develop and implement programs for themselves.

Skew Spending to Accomplish Corporate Goals

Which of the tactical programs should be used? How much should be spent on each tactic? The case of a telecommunications company illustrates how reimbursement percentages can be tweaked to encourage retailers to promote corporate goals.

The co-marketing team first identified corporate goals and assessed the market at maturity. Second, they developed a strategy to utilize each distribution channel to maximize its relative importance in contributing to these goals. Then, they skewed spending to reinforce the desired marketing activity for each channel.

In Table 9.1, the marketing activities encouraged by the company's reimbursement percentages are shown by channel segment. Spending was allocated to:

- Encourage all participants to include the desired branding and competitive copy in their advertising. By doing so, retailers could earn an additional 25 percent reimbursement of the cost of ads.

TABLE 9.1 Reimbursement Rates

Ad Copy	**Exclusive**	**Nonexclusive**
National branding message and logo	75%	50%
+ local market competitive copy	100%	75%
Media	**Exclusive Agents**	**Nonexclusive Agents**
Print, Broadcast, and Outdoor	75–100%	50–75%
Direct Mail and Telemarketing	Up to 100%	Up to 50%
SPIFs	Up to 100%	Up to 100%
In-store Display Materials	100%	100%
Trade Shows	Up to 100%	Up to 50%
Training	Up to 100%	Up to 100%
Yellow Pages		
Group	100%	Ineligible
Individual (limited to 20% of co-op funds)	Up to 100%	Ineligible
Group Newspaper Promotion (national promotion)	100%	Ineligible
Product Buy Down (national promotion)	100%	Ineligible
Promotions-in-a-box	100%	100%
Promotional Merchandise (trinkets and trash)	75%	50%

(Source: ACS TradeOne Marketing)

Table 9.1 identifies the manner in which spending will be skewed between exclusive and nonexclusive retailers in the wireless phone category.

- Encourage exclusive agents to spend money to develop store traffic. They were offered a higher percentage of their cost for advertising and promotion.
- Encourage nonexclusive agents to use funds to promote in-store activity. They were offered a higher percentage of their cost for these activities.

In competitive store environments, manufacturers have two good options. One is to offer store personnel incentives to recommend the manufacturer's product. The second is to create display and promotional offers at shelf level to entice consumers.

The Co-Marketing Plan

The co-marketing plan is a formal document summarizing the goals, strategies, and tactics used to create a co-marketing relationship with a trade partner. It should contain:

- **Goal statement:** State the corporate goals and the appropriate translation into trade-marketing goals
- **Pertinent research:** Make a summary of the research learning, isolating key points that reflect competitive standing and channel partners' wants and needs
- **Measurement metrics:** Identify the specific accomplishments of the plan in terms of market data, sell-through results, and customer satisfaction and the measurement techniques that will be used
- **Tactics by channel:** Recommend the specific actions to be taken in each channel to best motivate the channel partners to participate in the plan
- **Guidelines:** State the marketing tactics for each channel and their reimbursement levels
- **Time line:** Make a timetable and critical path showing what needs to be accomplished and the time schedule for implementing the plan
- **Budget:** Identify the total cost of implementing the program including:

    expected payout levels

administration expenses
training expenses
measurement and tracking expenses

Designing Appropriate Program Guidelines

Program guidelines explain the rules of the co-op programs to participating customers. Traditionally, these guidelines have been very staid. Customers are instructed precisely on how co-op money may be spent and on the procedure for claiming reimbursements.

But guidelines often fail to enlighten retailers on the objectives of the program. This oversight is easily corrected. Guidelines should correlate each of the optional tactics with corresponding corporate goals.

As discussed in the previous section, payment schedules (e.g., reimbursement percentages) should also reflect this correlation with corporate strategy. Customers are more likely to support goals when they're offered more money to do so.

Such incentives can encourage retailing customers to:

- use key copy points or product visuals
- include product benefit or positioning copy points
- advertise during key seasonal times
- exclude competitors
- use desired price points
- adhere to MAP points
- use preferred advertising media

Take the time to develop a clearly communicated set of program guidelines. They are the brains of the co-marketing plan. Program guidelines deserve the time and attention consumer-marketing folks lavish on product brochures or TV commercials. It is helpful to test guidelines on salespeople and certain key accounts before finalizing them. It's much easier to take the time to make sure that your guidelines clearly communicate the goals of your program rather than to suffer through the confusion later. Channel partners will appreciate and respond to this extra effort.

The following matrix in Figure 9.4 illustrates the types of guideline requirements that might be appropriate to guide the usage of different marketing elements.

FIGURE 9.4 ABC Corp.

Co-Op Guidelines Quick-Reference

Activity Reimbursement	Expenses Covered	Requirements	Required Documentation
Print Newspaper, magazine circulars, inserts	Net space costs Color charges Printing cost (nonmailer flyers/inserts only)	At least six column inches for newspaper ads ABC competitive copy for maximum reimbursement ABC Corp. logo Logo sizes: 6–11 column inches/16-point logo 12–30 column inches/24-point logo 31–70 column inches/30-point logo 71+ column inches/48-point logo Must meet all logo requirements	Original, full-page tear sheet with publication name and date Original publishers' invoices Original printer's invoice
Radio (FCC-licensed stations)	Airtime Radio remotes	Spots can be 15, 30, or 60 seconds 30-second spots require at least two ABC Corp. mentions; 60-second spots require at least three mentions Feature ABC competitive copy for maximum reimbursement For radio remotes the announcer must mention a copy point once every 30 minutes	Original dated script including notarized ANA/RBA certification with original signature of station official Original station invoice
Television	Airtime	Spots can be 30 or 60 seconds 30-second spots require at least two ABC Corp. mentions; 60-second spots require at least three mentions Feature ABC competitive copy for maximum reimbursement 1/4 screen-size visual ABC Corp. logo must air for at least three seconds	Original station invoice Original dates script or tape
Outdoor Advertising	Space cost	ABC Corp. logo	Photo(s) of entire outdoor ad/billboard Original invoice(s)
Yellow Pages	Display ads only* Monthly listing costs*	Feature ABC competitive copy for maximum reimbursement Must meet all logo requirements	
Direct Mail	Print and supply costs* Postage* Mailing list*	Feature ABC competitive copy for maximum reimbursement ABC Corp. logo	Complete original mailed piece Original printer's invoice Original invoice for postage or post office cash register receipt Proven marketing results
Store Signage (Permanent indoor/outdoor)	Production cost* Installation and electrical hookup*	ABC Corp. logo	Photo(s) of entire stock signage Original invoice(s)

Figure 9.4 illustrates the types of guideline requirements for a co-marketing plan.

FIGURE 9.4 ABC Corp.

Co-Op Guidelines Quick-Reference (continued)

Activity Reimbursement	Expense Covered	Requirements	Required Documentation
Point-of-Sale (Counter cards, ceiling mobiles, endcaps, posters, and banners)	Display materials* Standard shipping*	ABC Corp. logo	Photograph of display Original invoice(s)
Trade Shows and Sponsorships	Cost of booth space rental* Ineligible costs include: Electrical costs, travel costs, and employee expenses	Retailer must be identified as "ABC Corp. Retailer"	Photo of trade show booth or sponsorship display Original invoices itemizing costs Proven marketing results
SPIFs (limited to 20% of per activation accrual)	Full cost of incentives	ABC corporate-sponsored SPIFs	Complete the SPIF claim form
Promotional Merchandise	Cost of merchandise*	ABC Corp. logo Your company's logo must be at least 40% larger than the ABC logo	Original sample or photo of merchandise or materials Original invoice(s)
Training	Training costs* Reasonable airfare expenses* Hotel*	ABC corporate-developed training only	Proof of attendance Original invoices reflecting covered travel expenses
Business Cards	Printing cost	ABC Corp. logo in the bottom left or right corner Your company's logo must be at least 40% larger than the ABC logo	Original sample of card(s) Original printer's invoice
Promotions-in-a-box (PIB)	Cost of marketing and promotional kits Standard shipping of kits Associated taxes Space cost Airtime	Program options include: –print ads –POS materials –direct mail –card deck –broadcast fax –promotional items	No claim required—funds will be automatically deducted from your co-op account Note: ad space cost must be claimed separately and is subject to "print" guidelines
Telemarketing	Agency Fees	Use a third-party agency	Original script Original invoice from third-party agency
Other Activity	Described above*	Retailers must be identified as "ABC Corp. Retailer"	Original samples of any advertising or promotional efforts

Non-reimbursable costs include production, discounts, rebates, taxes, finance charges, interest, and agency.
* Prior approval may be required at the option of the manufacturer.

(Source: ACS TradeOne Marketing)

Now that you have selected program types, assigned funding and reimbursement amounts to each type, developed goals and measurement tools, and written the program guidelines, it's time to prepare the show for the road. Launching the program includes building enthusiasm among the sales force and providing training so they can successfully implement the programs.

For Your Review

Step 3: Aligning Strategies and Defining Trade-Marketing Goals

Points to keep in mind:

1. Get the big picture of your current trade-marketing program:
   - What is the total amount of spending from all sources?
   - Who is in charge of that spending?
   - Through what avenues are your marketing messages reaching your consumers?
   - Have you been aware of all the marketing messages your program has been supporting? Or have your consumers been receiving discordant messages?

An important goal is to establish a permanent position for your product in the public's mind, e.g., McDonald's. And don't let your brand message be destroyed by unmanaged trade spending.

2. Look ahead and project your product line's marketplace at maturity:
   - Have you clarified the roles of each of your channels in view of the market at maturity?
   - Does each channel partner know how you expect them to promote your product?
   - Do your partners know how they are protected from their competition in your other distribution channels?

Your goal is to have your product available when and where consumers will buy it, and it should be in the form most appropriate for the particular occasion of sale.

3. Plan carefully to set appropriate goals for your co-marketing plan and develop tools to measure those goals:
   - Are you measuring and comparing sales of your products? Pre- and post-program? Between accounts?
   - Are you tracking your advertising, both by dollar value and by percentage of advertising that includes your desired branding message?
   - Are you aware of your program's usage, specifically what funds are being claimed and how much of spending is used in accordance with your preferred strategy?
   - Are you using regularly scheduled AA&U studies to gain customer satisfaction ratings?
   - Are you measuring your sales force's satisfaction by sending out research questionnaires annually?
   - Are you thoroughly capturing significant market data?
   - Are you checking all ads on record for possible misuse of trademarks and MAP guidelines?

Setting goals and measuring them will help your company establish a successful program.

Step 4: Building the Plan

1. Review the various tactical programs you can choose from to contribute to your co-marketing goals, and choose the appropriate tactical program for each channel.
2. Vary reimbursement levels in your programs to reward desired behavior, encouraging each partner to promote your corporate strategy.
3. Draw up your co-marketing plan, documenting your goals, strategies, and tactics concerning each of your trade partners.
4. Design program guidelines for each of your channels. Be certain that your corporate goals are clearly communicated, and incentives are included to encourage partners to support your goals.

10

Carrying Out Your Co-Marketing Plan

STEP 5 Launching the Co-Marketing Plan

The process of launching a co-marketing plan should resemble to some extent the process of launching a new product. The co-marketing launch should be orchestrated to communicate to trade partners the goals, the spirit, the commitment, the excitement, and the messages of the program. Since it is the salespeople who will personally generate enthusiasm in and promote understanding of the program, the launch begins by preparing sales material for their use and a training program for them. The salespeople should be trained in the details of the program as well as persuaded to believe in its ability to improve customer relationships and consequently, sales.

Sales Materials

The following communication tools should be prepared to excite and educate both the salespeople and the trade partners:

- **Sales presentation**:
  Arm salespeople with materials that polish their presentations of the program. Develop a set of computer slides that graphically

communicate messages (using a program such as PowerPoint), and provide each salesperson with a copy of the disk. Build in ways that make it easy for salespeople to customize the presentation for each customer.

- **Customer leave-behind**:
  In addition to the guidelines, a leave-behind package must be created that communicates an overview of the program. It should be designed to cover everything from the strategy to the claiming procedures of the program. To encourage specific marketing activities, research data should be presented that demonstrates the success each activity has produced in the past. Particular attention should be devoted to those aspects of concern for the trade customer, namely the parameters of the program and claiming procedures. By emphasizing what is important to both the trade partner and the manufacturer, this leave-behind package will reinforce the spirit of cooperation that anchors the program.

- **Video**:
  A video may be produced to attract attention to the program in an entertaining way. Audiocassettes can also be helpful for salespeople who can listen while traveling between customer calls.

Sealy Mattress Company made especially good use of these tools. With the help of their co-op administration company, MediaNet, they produced a quick-reference guide that explained the co-op rules. The reference guide also included graphic examples of the "Top Five Claiming and Advertising Mistakes." This carefully researched list included the impact of each mistake on customer satisfaction and administrative cost.

To cement their relationships with their trade partners, Sealy produced a video script based on the *David Letterman Show*. In it, the "Top Ten Problems Customers Have with Co-op" was presented. Sealy salespeople could use the tape as a device to kick off talks about improving the account's business.

Salespeople left copies of the quick-reference guide behind so customers could refer to it when producing ads or making claims. The result of the Sealy program was a highly noticeable drop in customer complaints on claims. The polished communications campaign leveraged the program's chances for success.

Training for Success

Good salespeople share three traits. First, they are motivated to make something happen. Second, they trust and feel comfortable with the products or services they sell. Third, they protect their customer relationships.

A successful co-marketing program capitalizes on these characteristics. In Step 2, influential salespeople were interviewed to solicit input and build trust. Now it is time to build upon that foundation. The entire program depends upon salespeople who believe in it and will work proactively with their accounts. For this reason, they must be included in the final design of the program. The training should emphasize their ownership of the customer relationships as well as educate them about the program. Finally, it must convince them that the program will play an important role in their own successes.

Remember that the goal of co-marketing is to partner with the accounts. It is through the salespeople that this partnership is achieved. They must believe the co-marketing program is essential

A Strategic Investment Versus an Administrative Plan

In corporate America, developing and launching a new product generates much excitement. A dynamic, creative "product champion" coordinates the process. This manager reviews concepts with R&D types, brainstorms with the advertising agency, and evaluates test concepts and prototypes with market research personnel.

Despite the fact that fewer than 5 percent of new products are successful, executives spare nothing in their attempts to develop a winner. Hundreds of ideas are tested before one is judged good enough for full development. Hundreds of thousands of dollars are spent to develop prototypes and to market-research them with consumers. Finally, the product launch and accompanying promotional activities are planned.

It's no wonder that executives heap money and resources on the introduction of a new or redesigned product. These events place the business's entire management team under very bright lights. Executives understand there is no hiding from the judgments the trade, the press, and ultimately the consumer make on the idea and its implementation.

(continued)

A circus atmosphere often surrounds the new product launch, generating excitement throughout the company. The sales force receives thorough training on the features and benefits of the product; they learn how to present the product to prospective buyers. The salespeople are briefed on the marketing plan and their role in it. The product launch is a cause for anticipation and then celebration, eventually becoming an important milestone in corporate annals.

It would take quite an imagination to conceive of a co-op program receiving such fanfare. Co-op programs are not launched—they just dribble out. The development process consists of a couple of administrators writing some guidelines and circulating them among sales personnel for cursory comments. Once approved, the guidelines are assembled in a binder (sometimes three to five inches thick) and distributed to trade partners and the sales force.

Frequently organized like a set of assembly instructions written in four different languages, co-op programs are ambiguous at best. The ambiguity results from lack of attention. While an expert copywriter pens the prose for a new product launch, an overworked administrator bangs out guidelines for the trade-marketing program. The sales force, who should be expert at the program's contents, can't understand such guidelines even when they try. Predictably, the poorly conceived procedures and ill-advised presentation earn the guidelines a spot high on a shelf where they will rarely be consulted.

Salespeople respond to questions and complaints about the guidelines this way: "I don't know why they are the way they are. That's simply the way corporate wants it. They just don't understand what we're faced with out here. They don't know what it's like in the field where the business really takes place." To a large extent, such comments are right on target. The program becomes an administrative nuisance in which participants and salespeople must fight to have their claims paid. Harried administrators try to enforce confusing rules while personnel at key accounts, exasperated by the claims procedures, demand better treatment. When push comes to shove, the administrator usually backs down and allows these accounts to have their way.

If company executives truly intend for guidelines to improve understanding and cooperation between the manufacturer and the channel partner, they must approach the entire process differently. They must take an approach resembling the development and launch of a new product.

In light of its risks and rewards, executives may see the wisdom of investing more in their co-marketing program. For a very small investment, a successful co-marketing program can last for many years—assuming periodic tweaking. When approached carefully, its chances for success are 95 percent or better. And the improved trade relations that stem from a successful co-marketing program produce returns across all product lines.

This is not to imply that new product development should receive any less attention than it now receives. Rather, trade marketing should be more strategically managed than it currently is. In the long haul, these two endeavors will complement each other. The solid working relationships developed through a co-marketing program will create a receptive audience for new products.

not only to their company's success but to their individual success as well.

Training should demonstrate that the program will promote better relationships and generate better sales figures. When training salespeople in the use of a new co-marketing plan, five areas need to be covered:

1. the marketing strategy of the organization
2. the marketing needs of the retail accounts
3. branding and its importance to both the manufacturer and the retailer
4. how the co-marketing plan builds value and helps sales
5. customer objections and appropriate responses

Once the marketing materials have been developed and the sales force has been trained, it is time to move on to the next step of the Co-Marketing Solution: program administration and data capture.

STEP 6 Administering the Program and Capturing Data

Like a chain, the Co-Marketing Solution is only as strong as its weakest link. In the world of trade marketing and co-op advertising, administration is often that weak link. Weaknesses in this area lead directly to severe customer-satisfaction problems. The Co-Marketing Solution recognizes that weakness and addresses it.

Customers who are frustrated by the claims approval process are unlikely to cooperate enthusiastically in planning promotional activities. In fact, unhappy customers are likely to "punish" the unsuspecting and innocent salespeople. Appointments may be refused and new product deals may be ignored. This state of affairs is counterproductive for both the manufacturer and the trade partner.

Unfortunately, this state of affairs is the norm for most traditional co-op programs. The tide can be turned, however, by providing trade partners with a high level of "customer satisfaction" during the claims process. The following steps will ensure such satisfaction:

1. Issue program guidelines that are clearly written and easy to understand.
2. Provide information to customers in the form they prefer to receive it. This may include:
   a. a help desk to answer questions
   b. an integrated voice response (IVR) system so customers can access data anytime they want, via telephone
   c. Internet access to data
   d. dial-up modem access to data
3. Issue hard-copy monthly reports to each participant. These reports should tell them where they stand in the program and include:
   a. available funds that can be spent
   b. status of claims currently in the system
4. Set goals, and track the important dynamics of delivering the administrative service. Such data could include, but is not limited to:
   a. the percentage of phone calls answered within three rings
   b. the percentage of customer questions answered on the original phone call
   c. the percentage of customer questions answered within 24 hours
   d. the amount of time required to update the database to reflect new purchases
   e. the number of days into the new month needed to issue reports
   f. the percentage of customers expressing a problem with the program
   g. the accuracy of the data being reported
   h. the turnaround time for issuing payments

Customer Satisfaction

The following are examples of the types of customer-service performance standards that might be adopted to measure and report agents' satisfaction with the co-op program administration:

- **Prior approval turnaround:**
  Process prior-approval requests within two business days and offer an expedited same-day service under special circumstances.

- **Claim turnaround:**
  Process claims within 10 working days of receipt.

- **Payment process:**
  Generate checks and other documents weekly to two times a week depending upon how important cash flow is to your participants.

- **Phone calls:**
  a. 95 percent of all phone calls should be answered within 15 seconds.
  b. 95 percent of all phone calls should be resolved during the initial telephone call.
  c. 95 percent of all phone calls requiring investigation and follow-up should be responded to within 24 hours.
  d. 95 percent of all phone calls needing to be placed on hold should be on hold for a maximum of 30 seconds.

- **Reports:**
  a. Nonaccrual reports should be distributed no more than 10 working days after the first workday of the month.
  b. Accrual-based reports should be distributed to all audiences within 10 working days of receipt of valid monthly accruals with 100 percent accuracy.

- **Communication standards:**
  a. 100 percent spelling accuracy in all released correspondence.
  b. Weekly status reports should be generated to summarize the overall state of the program.

Data Capture

Prior to the advent of relational database technology, it was impossible to track the information required by the Co-Marketing Solution.

The MediaNet Story

Some marketing professionals at Texas Instruments back in the 1980s faced a problem. They wanted to track the various ways their retailers and wholesalers were spending Texas Instruments' co-op money. Research revealed no products were available that could both pay co-op claims and track how that money was being used.

In the entrepreneurial Texas Instruments culture, these marketers viewed this not as a problem, but as a business opportunity. They funded a start-up business to write software to pay and track retailer claims. It took about 18 months to develop, test, and prepare this program for sale.

But, as is often the case with software development, the market for the product turned out to be different from the one envisioned by the developers. The software was written to give small and midsize businesses the ability to organize and track trade spending in-house. But the first customers—Compaq and Frito-Lay—were large companies who wanted the benefit, but preferred not to perform this task themselves.

When the two giants sought a third party to administer the program, MediaNet, of Austin, Texas, was born. And so, the modern age of trade marketing began. John Langdon, one of the original founders, set out to make MediaNet into a claims-processing service for Fortune 1000 companies.

An ever-increasing appetite for marketing information fueled the growth of MediaNet. High-tech companies who began distributing their products through wider channels of distribution were especially anxious to harness and utilize market data. By the late 1980s, MediaNet was serving 15 clients—all Fortune 500 companies, and all attracted by the promise of unique marketing information.

Meanwhile, MediaNet's software was having a tough time keeping up with the demands of these clients. The need to process over a million claims per year and track multiple bits of information about each claim proved to be too big a job. After all, the original piece of software had been developed to handle one small or midsize company at a time.

The solution lay in relational database technology. This new type of computer processing allowed similar data to be stored together, thereby reducing the time it took to locate and access data. In a relational database, operating speeds increased dramatically. But that was not all. An extraordinary by-product of the new technology was the ability to conduct sophisticated analyses of the data. These analyses were just what MediaNet's customers ordered.

Executives at the small, privately funded business decided to go for it and undertook the massive project. In all, MediaNet invested three years and over $2 million to transition to relational database technology. Oracle, the leading database company, and Price Waterhouse, the Big Six accounting firm, were enlisted to design a new system specifically to pay trade-related claims and to capture details of those expenditures.

The investment paid off big when MediaNet signed Intel Corporation as a client in 1991. Equipped with its new high-tech database, MediaNet was able to help Intel produce the most visible co-op advertising program in the world. The Intel success attracted other companies to MediaNet, including IBM, Sealy Mattress, and Hewlett Packard.

Life on the cutting edge, however, was no bed of roses; it presented serious challenges for MediaNet. The data and analyses yielded by relational database technology seemed only to whet the voracious appetites of its giant customers. MediaNet's voyage on the cutting edge became a "bleeding edge." Useful analyses begot the need for even more analyses. As clients pored over the spending trends of their channel partners, their eyes were opened to the possibilities of even more sophisticated reports. The requests grew faster than MediaNet's ability to keep up with them.

Customers began to challenge the company with questions like, "How did my New York retailers spend their advertising this Christmas compared to last Christmas?" Clients reasoned that the information was contained in the database. They grew frustrated when MediaNet couldn't deliver analyses quickly. The ability to answer and trend such analytical questions still lay a few years down the road.

The problem was in the technology of database management and the design of high-speed processing applications. Built to record transactions efficiently, the database utilized a speedy data-capture technique called on-line transaction processing (OLTP). OLTP had helped Medialink (the name of MediaNet's database software) pay out over $1 billion each year. The software performed these transactions with superb data integrity and tight financial controls. But it was simply unable to analyze and trend data quickly. Such a piece of software must be easy to manipulate and to request information from. These types of design tools lagged a few years behind the development of the high-tech databases.

Confronted with the necessity for strict data integrity and the growing need for more complicated analyses, MediaNet executives looked for help. They called on me because of my experience with software technology and high-tech companies.

Analysis revealed that MediaNet was in its second metamorphosis. In its first, it had shifted from software provider to claims-processing service provider. Now, the company was being asked to become a provider of marketing intelligence as well.

The restructuring that is needed to meet a new and growing market demand is always painful. Fortunately, the management team at MediaNet immediately grasped the opportunity and made available ample resources for the restructuring. Eventually, the business was sold to Affiliated Computer Services (ACS) of Dallas, Texas, a $2 billion outsourcing company specializing in technology processing systems.

The continued use of state-of-the-art computer technology was assured through this wise move. In 1998, ACS acquired a second co-op processing firm, Pinpoint Marketing, and merged it with MediaNet to create ACS TradeOne Marketing, the largest third-party outsourcing company in the United States. This marriage of technology and market analysis is providing corporations the opportunity to consolidate and analyze their trade-market spending as they implement a fact-based selling system.

The enormous task of measuring, paying, and accumulating data on each retailer's advertising simply defied technology's best efforts until the early 1990s (see "The MediaNet Story").

Most of the valuable information captured in today's relational databases—like MediaNet's Medialink—can be found on the backup documentation that accompanies the claim for payment: the copy of the media invoice and a tear sheet of the advertisement. This backup material yields a great deal of market intelligence, including

- the spend category—the type of advertising, such as TV, radio, newspaper, and the percentage of spending each account allocates to that medium
- the advertising content of the ads
- which products are promoted and the percentage of spending allocated to each of them
- the promotional and sales materials each account uses and the quantities used
- the types of special promotions an account runs and the corresponding sell-through for each

The manufacturer is able to track how each account is spending its co-op funds. Category ads can be clipped to provide a source of information about how the same accounts are spending the competitors' co-op funds. Valuable determinations can be made from these data, including

- the share of advertising space by manufacturer and product
- promotional offers used to attract consumers
- advertised price points
- amount of space allocated to each manufacturer and product—to determine who has the dominant space in an ad

For Your Review

Step 5: Launching the Co-Marketing Plan

Forward-looking executives will regard the launching of a co-marketing plan as being similar to the launching of a new product:

- Are you prepared to invest an appropriate amount in your co-marketing program?
- Can both your salespeople and your partners clearly understand your program guidelines?
- Are you and your salespeople enthusiastic about the program and its projected results?

If you, your fellow executives, and your sales force strategically invest in and manage your co-marketing program, you will discover it will develop solid working relationships with your trade partners.

Step 6: Administering the Program and Capturing Data

Remember, the Co-Marketing Solution is only as strong as its weakest link, which most often is administration. The following tips address this weakness by concentrating on customer satisfaction:

- Issue program guidelines that are easy to understand.
- Provide information to customers in the form they prefer to receive it.
- Issue hard-copy monthly reports to each participant.
- Set goals, and track the important dynamics of delivering the administrative service.
- Ensure accurate and timely claim payment.
- Provide knowledgeable people for participants and salespeople to talk to.

11

Maintaining Your Co-Marketing Plan

STEP 7 Post-Analysis and Market Intelligence

If the co-marketing program is to continually improve, the research data collected in Step 6 must be analyzed so that it yields marketing intelligence. This process of deriving correct conclusions from the data depends greatly on the ability to formulate the proper questions. Thinking marketers who ask the right questions have the opportunity to make decisions that can improve sell-through and enhance the brand message. In addition to asking which retailer spent how much on which brand, marketers must study the messages and content of the ads run within the category. (This presupposes that competitive ads have been clipped.)

The relational database produces data on participating customers who submit claims. To stay abreast of competitors, clipped ads within the category must be tracked. By collecting all of this information, total category spending can be calculated, profiles for key customers can be developed, and promotional strategies can be monitored. Brand development can be compared with promotional ad spending.

Following is a series of questions that a marketing analyst may ask in an effort to stay attuned to the competition.

Tracking Competitive Advertising

"How is category spending split between different category segments?"

Figure 11.1 captures newspaper and circular spending within the wireless telephone category broken down by carriers and retail agents. The retail agents in this case may be small stores selling cellular services or national accounts. Over time, this analysis reveals spending trends for the category as well as for specific distribution channels or for individual retailers.

This analysis can help steer overall budget decisions. For instance, a company may decide it needs to increase spending in newspaper ads to maintain its share of voice (SOV). The analysis of spending patterns also reveals shifts in SOV over time, which leads to a second question.

FIGURE 11.1 Carrier Share of Cellular Category Print-Ad Spending

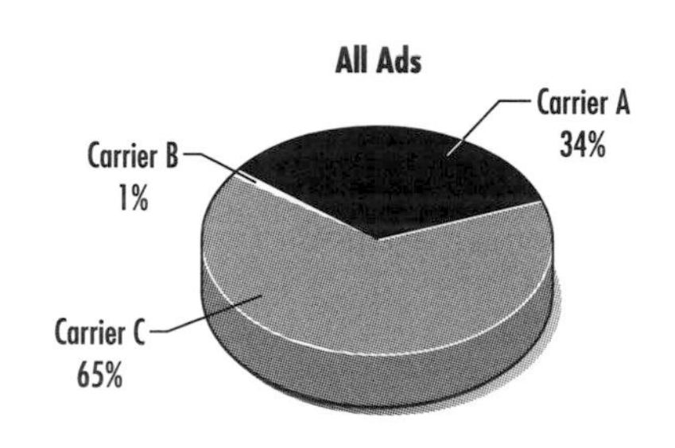

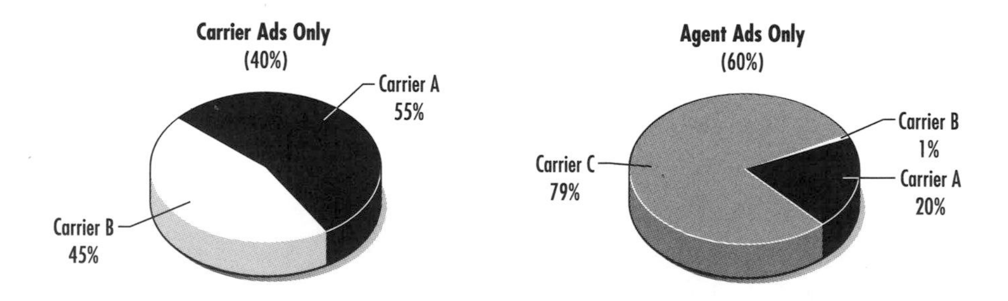

"What is the company's share of advertising spending in key accounts?"

Figure 11.2 captures the changes in wireless ad spending over one year. Again, the data are broken down into agents and carriers. This analysis reveals which manufacturers or brands are receiving the most support from a key account. Comparing this information to brand share can show a manufacturer whether their products are being under- or over-supported in retailer advertising, or their SOV.

In Figure 11.2, a huge one-year increase in print-ad spending is apparent in the carrier category. Executives who did not recognize this change would fail to pump additional dollars into their advertising budgets and would lose SOV as a result.

"How are the company's high-potential accounts promoting the company's products?"

Figure 11.3 depicts how major accounts divide up their newspaper advertising between brands. It also captures the changes in each manufacturer's share of advertising space over a one-year period. By understanding the support retailers are giving to various brands, executives can make decisions accordingly. Or perhaps they must ask more questions.

FIGURE 11.2 Wireless Print-Ad Spending Trends in Top 20 Cellular Markets

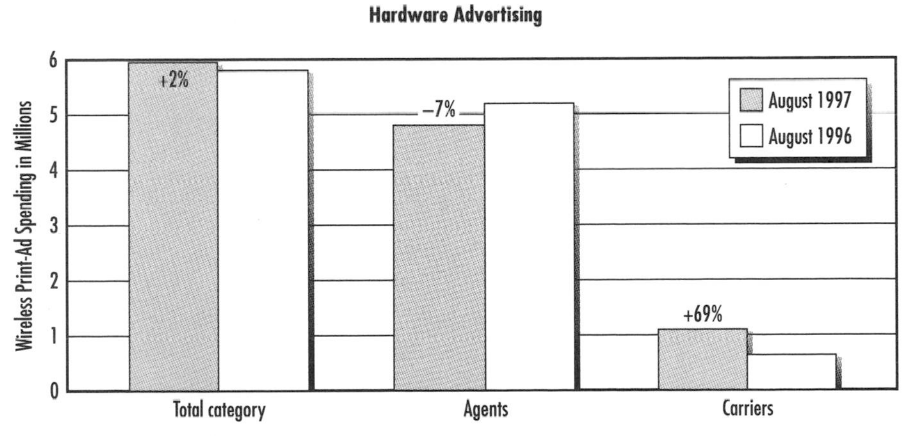

(Source: ACS TradeOne Marketing)

FIGURE 11.3 Hardware Ad Spending Trends Among Top Advertisers

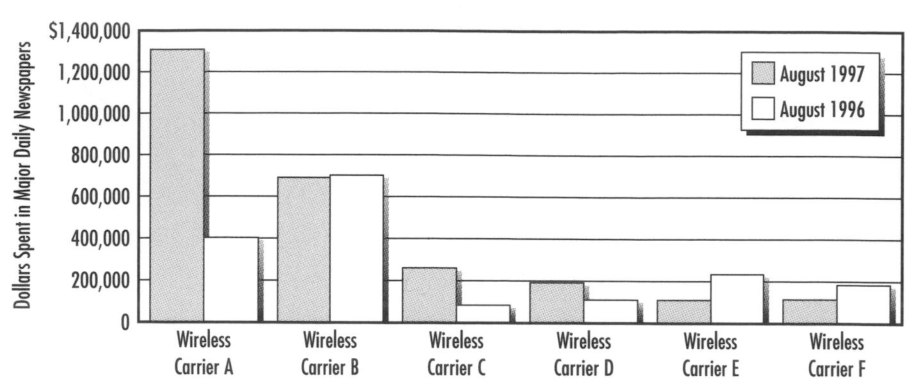

Wireless Carrier A's dramatic rate of growth far surpassed that of all other agents, but it still could not reverse this channel's spending decline.

(Source: ACS TradeOne Marketing)

"What are the main products being advertised?"

Table 11.1 depicts trends of brand advertising for major corporate and private label products.

TABLE 11.1 Top Agent Brand-Advertising Trends in Top 20 Wireless Markets

Changes in Brand Support (August 1997 versus August 1996)

	Ericsson	Motorola	Panasonic	Nokia	Sony	Private Label
Radio Shack 8/97	8%	2%	0%	23%	47%	6%
Radio Shack 8/96	2%	21%	0%	13%	0%	62%
Circuit City 8/97	19%	44%	0%	21%	12%	0%
Circuit City 8/96	1%	50%	45%	0%	1%	0%

While Radio Shack reduced its private label and Motorola support in favor of Sony and the PCS marketplace, Circuit City dropped Panasonic from its ad plan and shifted support to Ericsson, Nokia, and Sony.

(Source: ACS TradeOne Marketing)

Knowing which products are normally featured in retail advertising can help a manufacturing executive decide which products to promote and at what price points to promote them.

Analysts reviewing Figure 11.4, which captures the top six most advertised phones, would find that the Cell Phone A received more than twice the advertising support by retailers than its nearest competitor. Warning lights began blinking and forced executives to consider some changes in their advertising budgets.

"What offers are my competitors making to attract consumers?"

This analysis tracks primary consumer offers, including their rates and the trends with which they are used. In this way, a marketer can determine what it takes to be competitive and prevent overspending (e.g., through making consumer offers more lucrative than they need to be, or through advertising promotional offers that are not competitive).

Figure 11.5 illustrates how the frequency and trends in consumer offers can be tracked by analyzing category advertising. Phone purchase offers and unlimited local calls promotional offers top the rankings. These clearly represent the competitors' thrusts, and the

FIGURE 11.4 Top Phone Models—Carrier Ads Only

All Regions Combined: Models' Share of Total Agent Ad Spending

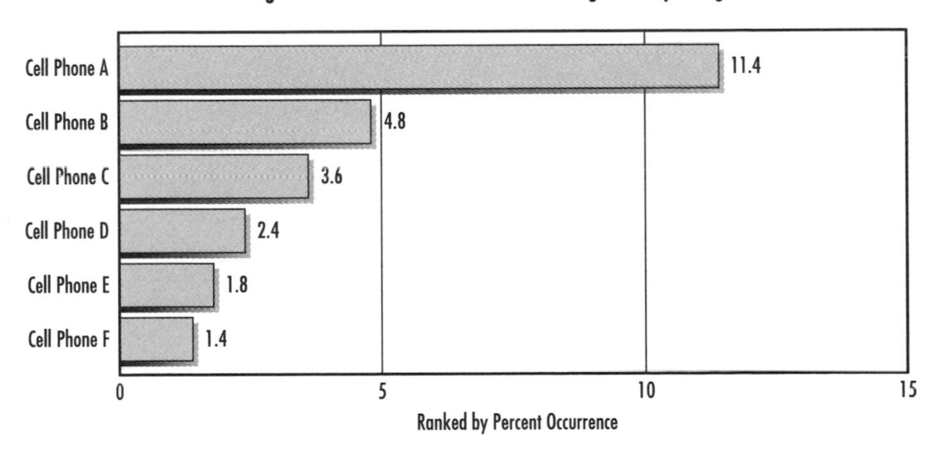

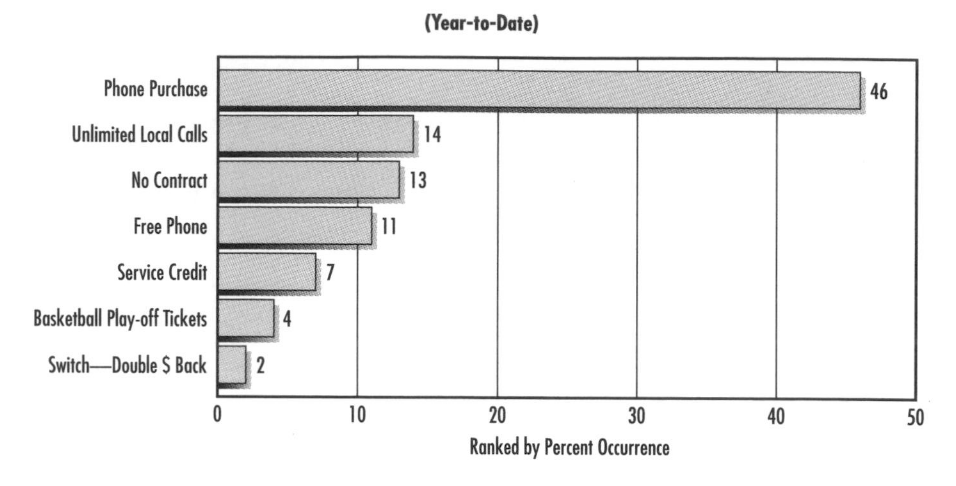

marketer should acknowledge these in developing the marketing plan.

Figure 11.6 depicts the offers carriers made month-by-month over a one-year period. Observe that phone purchase offers declined while offers for free nights and weekends increased. Knowing what the competitive trends are can help the marketer identify those that might need to be addressed.

The marketer can ask a number of other questions about competitive advertising, including:

- **Is co-op advertising contributing to sales?**
- **What price points are driving demand and how are the company's brands faring in light of these price points?** This data can help a marketer determine which price points to encourage retailers to take when negotiating for a temporary price reduction.
- **Are retailers using the advertising money given them on advertising?** Of course, this helps a manufacturer validate that they are receiving the ad support they are paying for.
- **Are a manufacturer's products receiving the best price features?** This helps a marketer evaluate the quality of the

FIGURE 11.6 Carrier-Offer Trends

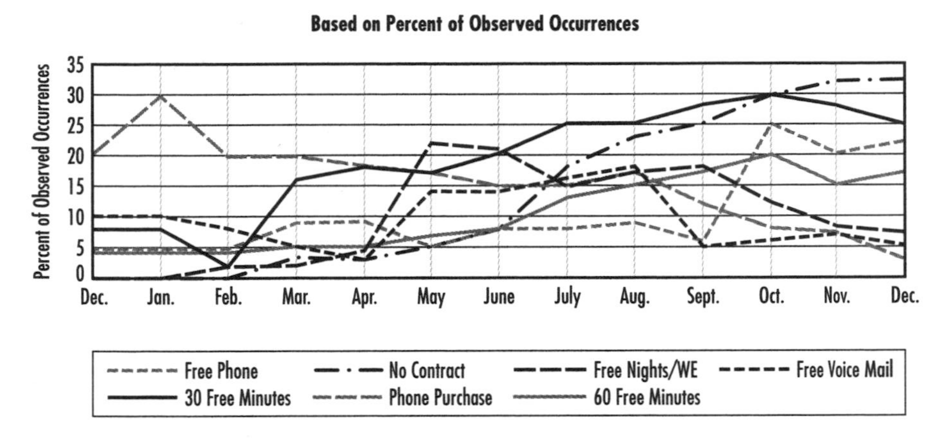

promotional support a product is receiving compared to the competition.

- **Are the manufacturer's products receiving a fair share of retailer advertising support?** This helps the manufacturer compare the share of advertising support to their share of sales within that account.
- **Which retailers are increasing or decreasing their advertising spending?** The answer to this question provides a sign of advertiser strength.
- **What promotional offers are competitors running?** This helps define the offers consumers are seeing to determine what level of offer a manufacturer might use to stand out.

Now the marketer must study how program participants are spending their co-op funds.

Analysis of Participant Spending

Data on participant spending, messages, and promotions are a gold mine of marketing intelligence. Correlating this data with sales can lead to significant conclusions about how to best promote a company's products.

Called sales growth profiling, this analysis charts the marketing efforts of wholesale and retail accounts, comparing the fast-growth accounts with average- and low-growth accounts. (This analysis presupposes that spending trends, advertising messages, and price points have been captured for each account.)

For the sales growth profile, each account is placed into one of three groups based on their actual sales results during the preceding 6-month or 12-month period:

1. fast-growth accounts
2. average-growth accounts
3. slow-growth or declining accounts

By distilling the spending patterns and types of advertising used by fast-growth accounts, marketers possess intelligence that can boost sales for other accounts. Figure 11.7 is a sales growth profile for a fictional company. It illustrates the type of analysis that can be accomplished and the type of communication that can be made through the sales force.

The first set of bars under each product indicates the fast-growth dealers. The second bar shows the average-growth dealers, and the third bar shows the slow-growth dealers.

As discussed in Chapter 4, Sealy Mattress Company used the sales growth profile to establish the optimum advertised price points for its mattresses (see Figure 4.4, page 72). The analysis revealed that advertising the $99 price point for a twin bed mattress and $499 for a Posturepedic produced high growth. This strategy was then passed on to dealers.

By relating sales growth to market factors such as product, price, and ad content, the data can be segmented to study other elements, including

- total spending by media
- use of trade shows and special events such as golf tournaments
- large accounts versus midsize and small accounts in overall dollar volume
- regional differences
- spending patterns by class of trade

FIGURE 11.7 Sales Growth Profile

Spending by Media

(Media spending as a percent of overall: January 1, 1997–December 31, 1997)

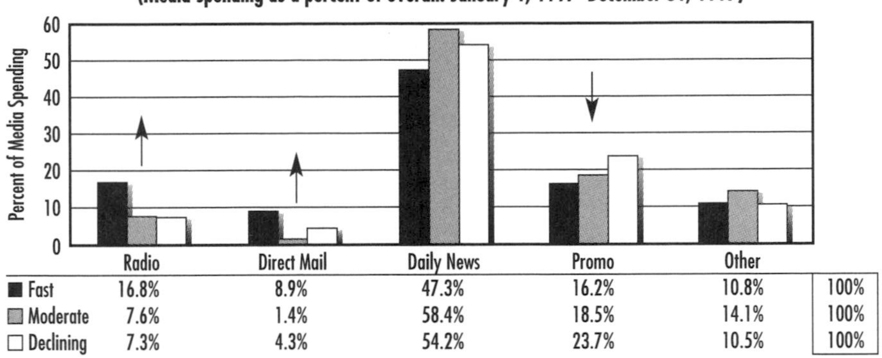

	Radio	Direct Mail	Daily News	Promo	Other	
■ Fast	16.8%	8.9%	47.3%	16.2%	10.8%	100%
▒ Moderate	7.6%	1.4%	58.4%	18.5%	14.1%	100%
□ Declining	7.3%	4.3%	54.2%	23.7%	10.5%	100%

Spending by Product

(Spending by product as a percent of overall: January 1, 1997–December 31, 1997)

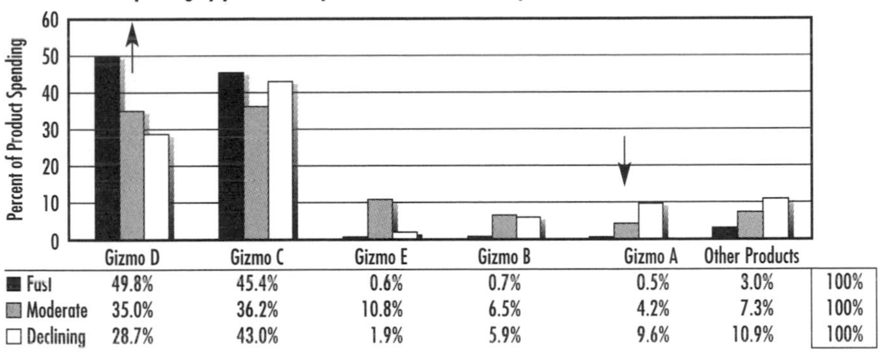

	Gizmo D	Gizmo C	Gizmo E	Gizmo B	Gizmo A	Other Products	
■ Fast	49.8%	45.4%	0.6%	0.7%	0.5%	3.0%	100%
▒ Moderate	35.0%	36.2%	10.8%	6.5%	4.2%	7.3%	100%
□ Declining	28.7%	43.0%	1.9%	5.9%	9.6%	10.9%	100%

Summary of Findings

Relative to the declining dealers, all growing dealers

- ▲ spend more money in radio advertising
- ▲ spend less money in promotional items
- ▲ advertise gizmo A less often
- ▲ advertise gizmo D more often
- ▲ show a picture of a gizmo more often
- ▲ advertise a free accessory more often
- ▲ advertise benefits more often

What to Do to Increase Your Sales

The fastest-growing dealers grew over 95% in one year, which is significantly faster than the rest of the dealers. Convince your customers to behave more like the fastest-growing dealers, and you will sell more product to them because they will sell more product to end users.

- ▲ Encourage your customers to explore and use radio advertising. Radio ads should carry both features and benefits copy to yield the best results.
- ▲ Encourage your customers to advertise the more advanced products, such as gizmos D and E. The fastest-growing dealers are leading the market's shift as they advertise these products more.
- ▲ Encourage your dealers to exhibit a picture of a gizmo, particularly when advertising the newer models.
- ▲ Motivate your customers to consider a promotional giveaway such as a free accessory. A free offer appears to be driving sales more successfully than the low-priced gizmo.
- ▲ Encourage your customers to moderate the amount they spend on "trinkets and trash," as excessive spending appears to yield negative returns. Money should be redirected to sales-driving media.

(Source: ACS TradeOne Marketing)

Clearly, a manufacturer equipped with well-documented marketing intelligence can influence how some accounts spend co-op funds. Performing a complete review of spending patterns and sales effectiveness every six months is highly recommended. Each time an element or combination of elements that correlates with sales growth is identified, the sales force should be informed so that they can pass on the intelligence to their accounts. Each year, program guidelines should be revised to reflect the intelligence accumulated over the course of the year. As discussed in the previous chapter, the manufacturer can encourage retailers to follow newly discovered high-growth strategies with incentives (e.g., paying a higher percentage of the cost).

Case Studies

In addition to competitive advertising tracking and sales growth profiles, marketers also can employ case studies to communicate marketing intelligence. Case study analyses help isolate trends that affect sales. They provide a systematic approach for capturing successful promotions. Case studies look beyond the numbers and isolate actual examples where an account has created an effective promotion. They showcase certain dealers and recognize their successes.

More Effective Promotions

When you identify the promotional elements that are driving sales, you are in a position to capitalize if you can communicate what you've learned to other channel partners in time. Today's markets are changing quickly, so it is necessary to communicate what you have learned and make it easy for other channel partners to re-create the dynamics. One of the best ways to do this is through proactive promotion planning and implementation support. Essentially, you have discovered through analysis what a few dealers are doing to promote sales effectively. Your goal is to get as many dealers in your network using this same tactic before the competition discovers it. Promotions-in-a-box is a method based on mass customization incorporating the marketing dynamics you wish to emphasize into a theme promotion. Materials comprised of direct mail, newspaper,

Case Study

Agent Background

Smith Communications is an ACME Wireless agent with four stores and a couple of kiosks located in the Luckenbach area of central Texas. It is a communications retailer that was founded in December of 1995 by a former ACME Wireless commercial accounts executive, Hondo Crouch. Through its three stores in October of 1997, Smith was signing up about 200 ACME Wireless customers a month. The agent was doing mostly radio advertising, mixed with occasional print ads in daily newspapers and some trade show efforts. Hondo positioned Smith Communications as a provider of "inexpensive phones and quality service."

Scenario and Goal

Smith Communications was opening its fourth store in a choice retail center in Fredricksburg, an upper-middle-class city of Gillespie County. Smith not only wanted to build awareness of and drive traffic to its new store, but also to generate more traffic at all of its stores during the important holiday season.

Smith Communications Radio Ad

(the first of four ads used)

WOMAN: So, Honey, where did you get that new cellular phone?

MAN: I got it from Smith Communications, an authorized agent of ACME.

WOMAN: Well that's a great looking phone. I'll bet you paid a fortune for it.

MAN: No, way! With my new ACME service agreement, I got a new ABC 900 for only one penny!

WOMAN: No way!

MAN: Yes way! Smith Communications is having a "One Penny" sale to celebrate the grand opening of its newest location in the General Store.

WOMAN: No way!

MAN: Yes way! These guys are everywhere. Not only are they now in Fredricksburg, they're also in the upper level of the Luckenbach General Store, The Super Kmart in Johnson City, the Flea Market Mall in Johnson City, and downtown Boerne.

WOMAN: No way!

MAN: Yes way! Not only that, but I also got ACME's "Save Me" 24-hour emergency roadside service.

WOMAN: Wow! You did get a great deal. So, since we saved all that money at Smith Communications, now you can start buying Christmas gifts for me!

MAN: No way.

WOMAN: Yes way.

MAN: No way.

WOMAN: Yes way. (Repeat and fade)

DISCLAIMER: "Offer available on select analog rate plans. Subject to one-year service agreement, credit approval, activation fee, and early cancellation fee. Other restrictions apply."

Case Study (continued)

Decision and Action

Smith chose to stick with radio, its tried-and-true medium, but it ventured out by attempting humor in its ads. Inspired by an acclaimed *Saturday Night Live* skit, Hondo decided upon a "No Way–Yes Way" angle that wrapped around messages announcing the grand opening of the new store, and presenting the regular offer of "the one-penny phone." The entire promotion this time was:

- An ABC 900 for 1¢ with a one-year service agreement
- A second ABC 900 for $9.95, and a companion line for $9.95 a month

Smith spent about $9,000 running three to nine ads a day, six days a week from mid-November to the end of the year. The agent placed four different, 60-second spots on two radio stations that reached its target market.

Result

The successful radio campaign "put [the new store] on the map," claims Hondo Crouch of Smith Communications. The humor in the ads got people's attention and the compelling offer of the one-penny phone elicited a response. Smith had three to nine people a day visit its new store in Fredricksburg during the campaign. Smith executives expected to activate two to four new customers a day at the new store, and they did, sometimes even signing up eight to ten a day! The other three locations also saw increased foot traffic from the advertising.

Over the 6-week holiday season, Smith Communications activated about 370 new customers, and Hondo attributes about 100 of those activations to the radio campaign. Hondo feels the phone offer and the frequency of the ads were the biggest reasons for the success, but the humor definitely helped. So much so that Smith continues to incorporate a humorous twist in its latest campaign. Hondo is a strong believer in advertising, and from his experience with this campaign, he advises others to "have ads be light-hearted, but don't lose the point." Seems like Smith Communications has figured out what works in central Texas: six months later, the Fredricksburg store is doing well, and Smith is preparing to open its fifth store in Sisterdale.

(Source: ACS TradeOne Marketing)

radio, and in-store materials are developed to the 85 percent completion level. The final 15 percent is custom-tailored to the desire of each trade partner. This allows channel partners to add their own strategic messages to the promotion or possibly an extra offer that is important within their market areas. The promotion is then ordered through a promotion planning desk that is set up to help the dealer plan the best delivery of the promotion to suit their budget. After the promotional copy is finalized, the promotion planning desk implements the promotion for the dealers by doing one or more of the following:

- ▲ completing the ads and sending camera-ready, properly sized materials to the dealer for placement
- ▲ placing ads in specified media
- ▲ buying the mailing list; printing and mailing direct-mail pieces
- ▲ drop-shipping store materials to each store
- ▲ providing radio scripts to local agencies or radio stations

Using corporately approved promotional themes and graphics, and customizing them for each dealer, has the decided advantage of encouraging sell-through activity that analysis has proved to be effective. Making it easy for dealers to implement using a promotional planning desk encourages dealers to take advantage of the ease of use. Furthermore, dealers begin to appreciate the manner in which you support the sale of your product through their stores and make it easy for them to do something that will generate demand.

Imagine the competitive advantage when analysis reveals an effective promotional offer (for example, see Figure 11.8), and four weeks later, prepackaged promotions are available for implementation. This type of turnaround time can greatly increase the effectiveness of promotional spending, increase sell-through, and build market share.

STEP 8 Rapid Action and Continuous Improvement

Using analysis of the gathered data to continually improve a trade-marketing program is the hallmark of the Co-Marketing Solution. Intel executives used the principles of the sales growth profile to achieve

FIGURE 11.8 Share of Wireless Category Promotion Offers

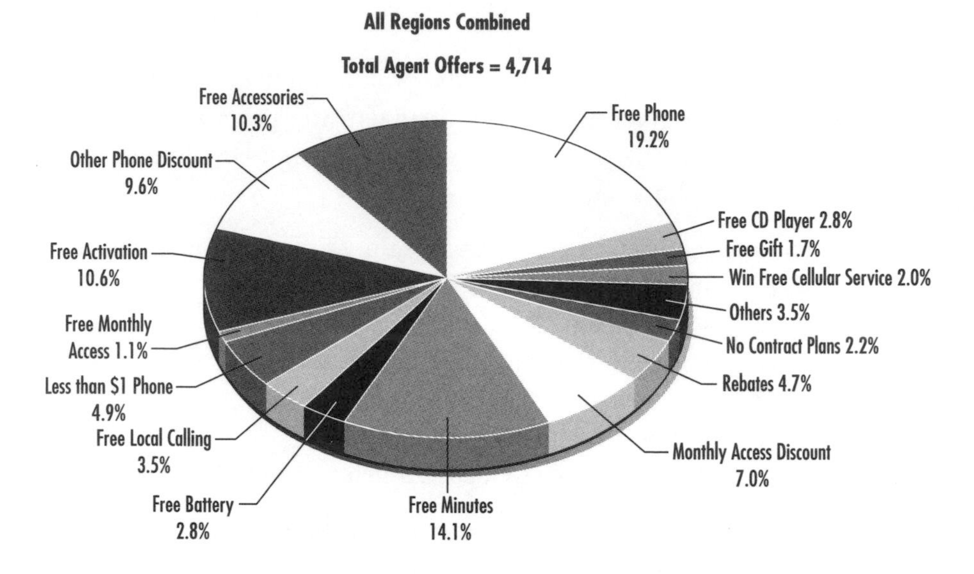

continuous improvement in their wildly successful co-op program. The way in which Intel management continually improved the program stands out as one of the most remarkable aspects of this campaign.

In the fourth year of the Intel Inside program, a sales growth profile was conducted. Analysis of that profile revealed that the fastest-growing customers were advertising on TV. Up to that point, most computer advertising had been confined to the print media (newspapers for retailers and magazines for manufacturers).

When analysis revealed that TV advertising generated superior sales results, Intel management revised their program guidelines. TV ads were reimbursed at an increased rate of 66 percent, compared to their standard rate of 50 percent.

Intel also developed a mnemonic device, a series of tones they wanted associated with the Intel name. They required their customers to use that device whenever the Intel name was mentioned in a TV ad. The tones were a stroke of genius. With just a visual message, the Intel name would probably have gone unnoticed. But the powerful auditory message drew attention to the name and dramatically increased consumer awareness.

Intel now ranks as one of the top-ten brand names among consumers. That's not bad for a computer microchip company that had virtually no consumer awareness in 1990!

Manufacturers have a variety of tools at their disposal to monitor their co-op programs:

- ▲ Attitude, awareness, and usage (AA&U) research track participants' attitudes and wants.
- ▲ Periodic sales-growth profiles isolate what the more effective retailers are doing to promote sales.
- ▲ ROI analysis provides the relative effectiveness of different spending alternatives.

Continually evaluating the co-marketing program creates an effective way to measure the program's effectiveness and to improve its performance every year.

In addition to the analysis of data, a change in management culture is also necessary if the full benefit of the co-marketing solution is to be realized. Two basic attitudes must be overcome in many companies. First, the belief that trade marketing is not strategic and therefore not worthy of top management's time and attention. Second, the lack of direct control when working through with channel partners relying on use of information to influence decision making rather that just telling someone what to do as is possible when working with consumer agencies.

Co-Marketing and the Organization Chart

Administrators—usually in the finance department or the sales department—traditionally manage co-op advertising programs under the credo, No news is good news. Efficiently paying claims is their prime focus. Bad news arises only when an important account has not received reimbursement in a timely fashion. If payment is made quickly, controversy is avoided. That's about as good as it gets for those administering co-op programs.

Most executives consider co-op programs as nothing more than a cost of doing business. As such, corporate resources are rarely lavished on those administering co-op programs. They are understaffed and overworked, like others in most cost centers. Under such conditions, anything beyond an effective claims payment system is highly unlikely.

It is no wonder that the idea of tracking marketing data simply does not come up. Executives view tracking systems as too costly both in terms of money and time. It is not unusual for most claiming systems to rely on generic spreadsheet programs, like Lotus 1-2-3.

Elevating Co-Marketing to Brand Status

While administrators in sales or finance oversee traditional co-op advertising programs, the planning arm of the business takes charge of the co-marketing program. Co-marketing earns this high-level supervision through its role as a source for marketing intelligence. Strategic planners also recognize the value of coordinating consumer and trade strategies as they attempt to deliver a consistent brand message (and to minimize messages that might erode the brand).

A co-marketing person may be given the title of Trade-Marketing Manager. Duties may include developing, implementing, and analyzing the co-marketing plan. While an administrator may still manage the function of processing claims, the trade-marketing manager handles the co-marketing strategy.

In this way, co-marketing rises to the level of brand planning. It is only at this level that the full benefits of co-marketing can be realized.

Perspective . . . Use It or Lose It

Some manufacturing executives ask me to straighten out their trade partners and to ensure that they remain under control. These executives often feel that their trade partners are abusing and even cheating them. "This is our money and it is being taken from us with precious little regard for our needs," they say. Such executives want proof of indiscretion. Quite often they seek to punish the offenders.

I tell them that co-marketing will not make channel partners fall in line and observe manufacturers' rules. It doesn't work that way.

The retail and wholesale community simply possesses too much power. They are not about to roll over and blindly comply with manufacturers' programs. In co-marketing, the goal is to advance strategic relationships with as many accounts as possible. It is unrealistic to expect 100 percent of the channel partners to participate at the strategic level.

In the absence of a co-marketing program, executives should expect perhaps 5 percent of their channel partners to be fully supportive of the manufacturer and its product lines. But an effective co-marketing program—one that clearly presents the manufacturer's strategy and the best way for the retailer or wholesaler to buy into it—can achieve participation up to 60 percent. It is virtually impossible, however, to achieve higher levels of participation, because channel partners have their own sets of needs, some of which may preclude strategic partnering.

Retailers or wholesalers experiencing a traumatic period (e.g., financial crisis or a management restructuring) may become myopic and refuse to engage in strategic partnering with any firm. In some organizations, the corporate culture simply precludes co-partnering.

On the other hand, many retailers and wholesalers are willing to partner with manufacturers. To determine which ones are willing, the manufacturer takes the lead in advancing the relationships. That means the manufacturer must undertake the chore of presenting the corporate strategy and the provisions of the program to as many accounts as possible.

What to do when a manufacturing executive feels mistreated? When should retailers guilty of insubordination be punished? Never. There is no room in the relationship between manufacturer and distribution partner for punishment. Wholesalers and retailers have something that manufacturers desperately need: shelf space to carry their products. If a manufacturer adopts a punitive attitude toward its channel partners, and many do, it will lose distribution outlets as some accounts fight back and drop the manufacturer's products. Nothing is accomplished and much is lost when this occurs.

While the co-marketing approach does not promote the use of punishments, it does measure the effectiveness of each customer. Sales and adherence to strategic program elements are rigorously tracked. Reports clearly identify the accounts that are participating strategically and those that aren't.

Tracking produces the information necessary to generate a spending profile and a corresponding market impact for each account. Such data can help salespeople demonstrate how some accounts have profited from strategic partnering with the manufacturer. Or the data may indicate that an account is not ready; efforts would be wasted on them at the current time. Spending profiles create a fact-based framework to help manufacturing executives decide how to work with each account.

By combining tools for measuring and reporting with a package of financial incentives, a manufacturer is prepared to reinforce the desired behavior. This ability to influence the behavior of trade partners creates the backbone of the Co-Marketing Solution.

I strongly believe that a co-marketing program should allow trade partners to do what they want; but the program also should encourage the *desired* behavior through higher reimbursement levels. This creates a tangible discussion point for salespeople to use with each account. By outlining each reimbursement level along with its strategic requirements, the salesperson sends a strong message to the buyer or merchandising manager: The manufacturer can afford to pay more for strategic behaviors because they have been proved to work.

Retailers and wholesalers may recognize that this is not the language of a traditional co-op program; the manufacturer doesn't view the program as merely a cost of doing business. Retailers will understand that the manufacturer is delineating the conditions under which the manufacturer is prepared to invest in the channel partners.

Each reimbursement level should be supported with facts (e.g., how a competitor's promotion generated record sales). Facts about how to promote and how to generate additional sales create a compelling argument for collaboration between manufacturer and customer. Knowledge is power. By bringing knowledge to the table, the manufacturer can transform an adversarial relationship into a mutually beneficial partnership.

Picking a Co-Marketing Agency

One of the most important decisions you make will be whether you manage co-marketing internally or use an outside agency to assist you. The economics favor seeking outside assistance. The database systems and accounting efforts usually demand a custom-designed system. This is expensive to design and program, thus favoring using a co-marketing agency that has already made this investment. Also, there is an enormous amount of experience and expertise required to make the most of the opportunities that co-marketing represents. After all, if co-marketing could increase the effectiveness of the dollars spent by only 20 percent, what an amazing return on investment that would be! Imagine what the Intel Inside program has meant to Intel!

Selecting a co-marketing agency is very similar to selecting an advertising agency. Most manufacturers elect to use an outside advertising agency if they can afford it, because they get objective outside opinions and a better creative product. The same is true of using a co-marketing agency, and then some. Not only is database technology daunting to most manufacturers, but also the marketers' experience working with retailers is usually lacking. It is also very helpful to have a third party involved in the claim payment and customer support functions working with the accounts. This provides some arm's-length objectivity when enforcing guidelines, and in the case of a problem, allows the manufacturer to step in and take the role of the good guy if desired.

When trying to find an agency to assist you in the relatively new field of co-marketing, you may want to keep the following factors in mind:

- **Systems capability:**
  The agency's systems should feature an industrial-strength accounting system with the capability to track additional marketing data. Remember co-marketing payments represent a substantial fiduciary responsibility that should be tracked with a complete audit trail following generally accepted accounting

principles. Additionally, the agency should be expert at reporting capability and the use of Web, integrated voice response, and business information software tools.

- **Experience:**
  The agency should have experience either in your channel or with a dealer channel that is very similar to yours. Strategic approaches to working with dealers and promotion planning should inspire you much the same way that an ad agency's previous creative efforts would help you to choose that agency. The "product" of previous co-marketing efforts should be carefully reviewed.

- **Personnel:**
  The personnel should include financial people to deal with the accounting aspects of payment, administrative people highly trained in customer support, and marketing and advertising people experienced in market analysis, promotion planning, and trade marketing.

- **Proactivity:**
  The agency must have a sense of urgency to find the market dynamics that drive sales, and the ability to recreate them quickly through targeted marketing programs made available to most dealers in a matter of weeks.

- **Technology:**
  The agency's management should understand technology and how to use it to drive a business. Technology is expensive to invest in and difficult to manage unless a very clear understanding of its purpose is communicated. Proven skill in the evolving area of on-line analytical processing and the ability to analyze data quickly to find relevant marketing information are crucial to good co-marketing.

When choosing an advertising agency, price is a secondary consideration. In fact, low-priced vendors should rarely, if ever, be considered. This is because the value of the work done right far overcomes the cost. In the world of consumer advertising, fees typically run from 10 to 17 percent of media dollars spent. In the world of co-op claims processing, fees run about 3 percent of money paid. Obviously, most people buying claims processing are not looking for the value that co-marketing can provide. Given the importance of the dollars being spent in the trade area and the fact that they are more measurable suggests that a manufacturer should be willing to spend, at the low end, 10 percent of what is invested in managing the consumer-marketing budget.

A new kind of agency is called for that combines the marketing and research expertise found in the consumer world, the financial processing capability found in co-op processing, the promotion planning capability of a promotions agency, and the advertising experience of an ad agency. This new type of agency is the co-marketing agency.

One final word of advice: If you do choose to work with an outside co-marketing agency, treat them as a strategic partner. Introduce them to your consumer agency. Include them in business reviews and strategic planning sessions, and communicate branding goals to them. Seek their input and advice when it comes to your marketing strategies. Do everything you can to make them an equal partner in the delivery of your marketing messages.

Whether you decide to implement the Co-Marketing Solution in-house or with the help of an outside agency, the value this approach can provide will be nothing short of amazing.

Good luck and good co-marketing!

For Your Review

Step 7: Post-Analysis and Market Intelligence

Savvy executives realize the need to continually improve their co-marketing programs. Thinking marketers

- ask the right questions in order to make decisions that improve sell-through and enhance the brand message
- track competitive advertising in order to stay abreast of competition

- analyze how channel partners are using co-op funds, to determine which ones are growing fastest and why
- make sure marketing information and promotional materials are conveniently made available to channel partners

The goal is to get as many of your partners using the more-effective promotions before your competition does.

Step 8: Rapid Action and Continuous Improvement

Continue to evaluate your co-marketing program:

- Use AA&U research to track participants' attitudes and wants.
- Use periodic sales-growth profiles to isolate what promotes sales.
- Use ROI analysis to determine the relative effectiveness of different spending alternatives.

Gauge your company's attitudes toward the Co-Marketing Solution:

- Do they realize that trade marketing is strategic, and therefore demands top management's time and attention?
- Are they prepared to work together with channel partners, using information to show how the co-marketing plan will help them improve business, rather than expect partners to do as they are told?

Finally, if you decide to use an outside agency to manage your co-marketing:

- Make sure it is a competent agency with the appropriate systems capability, experience, personnel, proactivity, and technology.
- Remember price is secondary. After all, consider the size of your trade-marketing budget; that should convince you to get only the best to manage it.
- Treat your co-marketing agency as a strategic partner.

Glossary of Co-Marketing Terms

AA&U (Attitude, Awareness & Usage). A research survey to measure wants, needs, and perceptions.

Accrual. Funds set aside based on purchases and available for claiming; normally limited to a stated period of time for usage, i.e., accrual period.

Affidavit of performance. A sworn statement attesting to the placement of advertising, documenting time, place, cost, content, etc. Issued by the medium (TV station, radio station, etc.) where the advertising ran.

Audit. The act of physically examining a claim to measure it for size, compare to guidelines, and verify cost for reimbursement determination.

Brand marketing. The planning-based management system developed by Procter & Gamble to manage branded product lines based on product positioning, communication, and understanding consumer needs. Also referred to as consumer packaged-goods and product marketing due to its developmental roots in consumer packaged-goods marketing.

Branding. The art of making a product, service, or company stand for a given set of values in the mind of the end user.

Category killers. Large discount retailers like Wal-Mart and Home Depot who break the price levels of a product, making it hard for smaller retailers to compete.

Category management. Refers to the way retailers try to maximize category sales and profits by combining branded and private label products.

Co-branding. Combining brand names to create an end-user message that is greater than either of the individual brand images alone. Licensing and the use of the Eddie Bauer name by Ford to denote a fashionable interior package are examples of this marketing technique.

Co-marketing. The practice of strategic alignment between retailer and manufacturer to conduct joint-brand promotion.

Consumer advertising. Corporate funded, direct-to-end-user advertising usually developed by an outside advertising agency according to the strategy statement provided by client, i.e., manufacturer or service provider. Corporate has complete control of the advertising message and how it is presented to the end user.

Co-op advertising. The traditional practice of the manufacturer paying for a portion of the advertising or promotion cost a retailer incurs to promote a retail product. A tactical program implemented though the sales force.

Demographics. The tangible dimensions used to define a consumer or market target, i.e., age, sex, religion, race, household size and income, where they live, etc.

Direct marketing. Telemarketing and direct mail so termed because it is possible to target exactly who will be marketed to based on demographic or product usage profiles, as opposed to other marketing forms, like advertising, which broadcast the advertising message to all consumers present.

Display allowance. Payments manufacturers make to retailers for in-store displays or preferential shelf positioning.

Electronic tear sheet. The formal documentation electronic mediums (television, radio stations) issue to verify that a specific commercial script ran, on what stations it ran, how many times, and at what cost.

Exclusive dealer. One who carries only one manufacturer's product line.

Focus of sale. A part of the positioning strategy statement that defines the singular, most important point to communicate to potential buyers.

Free standing insert (FSI). Advertising delivered with a newspaper or magazine, but not printed at the same time as the periodical. Also referred to as circular or preprints. The term also refers to coupons sometimes added during binding to "pop up" between pages.

FTC Guides. The full name is the Federal Trade Commission Guides for Advertising Allowances and Other Merchandising Payments and Services. The guides present the commission's view of how suppliers, retailers, media, and other third parties can comply with the terms of the Robinson-Patman Act. They were issued in 1960 and reissued with modifications in 1969 after a Supreme Court decision in the case of *FTC v. Fred Meyers*. Hence, the guides are sometimes referred to as the "Fred Meyers Guides." The guides were reissued again in 1972 and 1990 with minor revisions.

Gross rating point (GRP). Method used to measure how many households are reached by a television campaign (series of commercials). Each GRP equates to 144 thousand households. See also reach and frequency.

Incentive plans. Programs that motivate the salesperson. See also SPIF.

Key account planning. Developing specific plans for each major account using a formal planning and approval process.

Market development funds (MDF). Promotional funds spent according to a joint plan or agreement to meet a strategic goal with a channel partner.

Media. Where advertising runs, i.e., television, radio, print (magazine, newspaper, etc.), and direct marketing.

Mood and tone. Part of the positioning strategy statement that expresses the appropriate tone of consumer communications.

Nonexclusive dealer. Retailer who carries competing manufacturers' product lines.

Nontraditional media. Spend options (which are frequently non-media) not available in co-op programs prior to 1980; for example, inventory financing, sales and service training, seminars, workshops, trade shows, and special events.

Omnibus ad. A retail ad that features more than one supplier. Also referred to as competitive ads.

Outdoor advertising. Billboards, stadium signage, and taxi and bus posters. Refers to locations where advertising is posted on a regular basis.

Pending. Practice of holding claim to pay the remainder due when available funds are earned rather than forcing participant to resubmit claim when funds are available for partial payment only.

Point of sale (POS). Marketing message or promotion at the shelf level.

Positioning strategy statement. Concise statement used to communicate the important branding elements. It is used to govern all consumer-level communication to ensure consistent application of branding message.

Preapproval. Practice of submitting materials for approval prior to their use in the marketplace. Also called **prior approval**.

Psychographics. Method of segmenting consumers according to values or lifestyle issues.

Push money. When manufacturers offer cash or other incentives to retailers' salespeople to induce them to recommend the manufacturers' products to consumers.

Rate. What the advertiser is charged. Most broadcast stations have only one rate (and most rates are negotiated based upon demand and availability). There are different rates for national and regional ("spot") buys. There are many different types of newspaper rates, among them:

Combination rate: rate for buying space in more than one edition, zone, newspaper, etc.

Commissionable rate: rate includes commission for advertising agency (usually 15 percent)

Local rate: rate paid by retail advertiser for space purchased in local paper

National rate: rate paid when buying space at the national level (usually higher than local rate)

Open rate: rate for advertising before quantity discounts for multiple insertions

Vendor rate: rate at which some retailers charge for cooperative advertising; ostensibly based on the rate paid by retailers plus overhead for managing the advertising process; in actuality, practice of charging more than rate card for advertising in order to make a profit

Reach and frequency. Method of measuring advertising effectiveness, especially TV, by calculating percentage of available households (reach) and the number of times each is reached (frequency).

Rebate program. Type of manufacturer discount which is automatically paid, based on sales, at the end of a given period.

Return of investment (ROI). The incremental sales dollars generated by a promotion divided by the cost of the promotion.

Robinson-Patman Act. Federal legislation requiring that all competing customers within a class of trade must be treated equally regarding pricing and discount structures.

Run of press (ROP). A newspaper's practice of placing an ad wherever in the paper the publisher desires.

Run of schedule (ROS). A broadcast station's option of running a commercial in any time slot it desires.

Sales incentives. Promotional incentives paid directly to the salesperson based upon performance.

Share of market (SOM). Percentage of total sales that a manufacturer or product enjoys.

Share of voice (SOV). Percentage of total advertising spending (weight) that a manufacturer or product enjoys.

Slicks. Camera-ready advertising templates.

Soft dollars. Promotional funds paid to retailer or distributor without any proof of performance, i.e., claiming.

SPIF (Sales Person Incentive Fund). Promotional payments made directly to the salesperson for performance. If over $600 is paid in a calendar year, a 1099 statement must be filed with the IRS.

Stock-keeping unit (SKU). Individual unit of retail inventory.

Storyboard. Pictorial view of each frame of a television commercial.

Target market. Element of the positioning strategy statement that identifies the target consumer from a demographic and psychographic viewpoint.

Tear sheet. In print media, the entire page in which an ad runs.

Trade loading. When a manufacturer induces the trade to take more product in stock than can be expected to sell through in a reasonable period of time, resulting in excessive inventory conditions.

Traditional advertising. Television, newspaper, and other media that has always been included in co-op advertising programs.

Unique selling proposition (USP). The statement expressing the competitive differences that characterize what a brand stands for.

Bibliography

Aaker, D. A. *Managing Brand Equity*. New York: Macmillan, 1991.

Branding. "Brand Equity." *BrandWeek*, 28 June 1993.

Houk, Bob. *Co-Op Advertising*. Lincolnwood, IL: NTC/Contemporary Publishing, 1995.

Jacody, Jacob, and Robert W. Chestnut. *Brand Loyalty: Measurement and Management*. New York: John Wiley and Sons, Inc., 1978.

Lefton, Terry, with Weston Anson. "How Much Is Your Brand Worth?" *BrandWeek*, 29 January 1996.

Ousuroff, Alexandra. "Brands: Who's Hot—Who's Not." *Financial World*, 2 August 1994.

Penrose, Noel. "Brand Valuation: A Management Tool for the 1990s." *The Advertiser*, Summer 1993.

Retailing. "Change at the Check-Out." *The Economist*, 4 March 1995.

Therrien, Lois, with Maria Mallory and Zachary Schiller. "Brands on the Run: How Marketers Deal with Eroding Loyalty." *Business Week*, April 1993.

Walker, Chip. "How Strong Is Your Brand?" *Marketing Tools*, January–February 1995.

Index

About the Author

Shawn Clark is the CEO of ACS TradeOne Marketing. He has been director and vice president of brand marketing at several Fortune 500 companies, including H.J. Heinz, Hunt-Wesson, Inc., J&J Pharmaceuticals, and RJR Nabisco. Clark has also worked with several prominent high-tech companies, including Intel, Texas Instruments, Motorola, Nokia, Adobe Systems, IBM, and GTE Wireless. He is a frequent speaker at trade shows and industry events on branding and trade marketing. He lives in Austin, TX, with his wife and family and can be reached at Sclark5604@aol.com or www.co-marketingsolution.com. He can also be reached by phone at (512) 343-2002, extension 431, or (512) 657-7833.

American Marketing Association

The American Marketing Association is the world's largest and most comprehensive professional association of marketers. With more than 45,000 members, the AMA has more than 500 chapters throughout North America. The AMA sponsors 25 major conferences per year, covering topics such as the latest trends in customer satisfaction measurement, business-to-business and services marketing, attitude research, and sales promotion. The AMA also publishes nine major marketing publications.